HANDBOOK OF WORK AND ORGANIZATIONAL PSYCHOLOGY

Volume 1: Introduction to Work and Organizational Psychology

HANDBOOK OF WORK AND ORGANIZATIONAL PSYCHOLOGY

(Second Edition)

Volume 1: Introduction to Work and
Organizational Psychology

Edited by

Pieter J.D. Drenth

Vrije Universiteit,
Amsterdam,
The Netherlands

Henk Thierry

Tilburg University,
The Netherlands

Charles J. de Wolff

Catholic University,
Nijmegen,
The Netherlands

Psychology Press
a member of the Taylor & Francis group

Psychology Press Ltd
27 Church Road
Hove
East Sussex, BN3 2FA, UK

British Library Cataloguing in Publication Data
A catalogue record for this title is available from the British Library

Volume 1
ISBN 0-86377-520-9 (Hbk)

Cover illustration by Clive Goodyer
Cover design by Rachael Adams
Typeset by Mendip Communications Ltd, Frome, Somerset
Printed and bound in the United Kingdom by Redwood Books Ltd, Trowbridge, Wilts, UK

Contents

Contributors to Volume 1

Charles J. de Wolff, Gomarius Messtraat 19, Alverna, 6603 CS Wychen, The Netherlands.

Pieter J.D. Drenth, Vrije Universiteit, Faculteit Psychologie en Pedagogiek, Van der Boechorststraat 1, 1081 BT Amsterdam, The Netherlands.

Sylvia Shimmin, 12 Strait Lane, Huby, Leeds LS17 0EA, UK.

Pieter J. van Strien, Elsschotlaan 26, 9721 WN Groningen, The Netherlands.

Henk Thierry, Katholieke Universiteit Brabant, Faculteit Sociale Wetenschappen, P.O. Box 90153, 5000 LE Tilburg, The Netherlands.

1

What is Work and Organizational Psychology?

Pieter J.D. Drenth, Henk Thierry and Charles J. de Wolff

In the first half of the 1980s, the *Handbook of Work and Organizational Psychology* edited by us—and by our deceased colleague Paul Willems—appeared, at first in Dutch and subsequently in an English translation. It was the first comprehensive handbook in this field on European soil, and the *Handbook* found a widespread market. Our discipline is developing rapidly, and the need for an enlarged and new edition of the *Handbook* became apparent. An enlargement was deemed necessary, as in many fields many new studies had been published and many interesting applications had presented themselves. A revision was required as some new topics deserved a separate chapter.

The present result has appeared, not as an updated book, but as a completely rewritten new *Handbook*. In this first chapter we will begin with a characterization of the domain of work and organizational psychology. Attention will be paid to its relations with other subdisciplines in psychology, and its relation with other disciplines that are also concerned with work and organization. In connection with this topic, a section deals with the

relation between pure and applied science. Following an exploration of possible or probable developments in work and organizational psychology in the (near) future, the chapter is concluded with a brief presentation of the organization of this new *Handbook*.

THE DOMAIN OF WORK AND ORGANIZATIONAL PSYCHOLOGY

Work and organizational psychology refers to the subfield within psychology that is specifically concerned with human behaviour at work in, or in connection with, a work organization. Three aspects characterize this description. First, it concerns the *behaviour* of *working people*. Behaviour is not only understood to mean directly observable work actions, but also intentions, attitudes, emotions, habits, motives, etc. of a person in work. In fact, behaviour at work comprises all actions and reactions coming from a worker that can be observed or derived from this behaviour. This is why in work and organizational psychology of old, much emphasis is laid on the importance of valid diagnostic instruments—such as tests and scales—and of proper methods of research (see also Chapter 2, this Volume). Many topics in work and organizational psychology relate to behaviour of the *individual* (and therefore to individual differences), such as selection, performance assessment, designing a career plan, support and advice in case of difficulties, etc. In other subject areas, however, individual differences among those employed remain a little more in the background and attention is focused on the behaviour of what we wish to call "sets" of people. Such a set may have the characteristics of a group, defined in a social-psychological sense—such as semi-autonomous or self-steering units in a company—but this is not necessarily the case. Consider topics such as (re)designing work tasks, enhancing productivity, flexibilizing employment conditions, reducing the chance of stress. The common element in human behaviour, then, is for example their position as employees in a work organization, the fact that they come under the same Collective Labour Agreement, or that they attend the same course or take the same training. It is true that work and organizational psychologists are concerned with human behavioural characteristics in relation to these topics, but not (primarily) with individual differences.

Second, we have the concept of employment or *work*. In a strict sense, work refers to the activities someone performs based on his or her position in a work organization and entitle him/her to an income or another financial recompense. This context applies to most topics in work and organizational psychology. But in addition, an increasing amount of interest has developed for topics relating to other forms of work. For example, it is important to know what interests and objectives pupils consider concerning their first position, how entrants to the labour market are made fully aware of the standards and values in their first company (socialization), how people suddenly confronted with dismissal can be motivated by devoting themselves to new challenges, how the elderly are prepared for the time in which they no longer have a job, and so on. More and more people will also (have to) adjust themselves

to having more than one career, constant further training and retraining and using leisure time meaningfully during intermediate "jobless" periods.

The third aspect, behaviour at work *in* or *in connection with a work organization*, demonstrates first and foremost that work is always part of a "regulated collaboration" with others. Work presupposes "organization", which means for example a social system with a structure consisting of distribution, assignment, coordination and control of tasks and people. Interesting work and organizational psychological research questions relate for example to an inherent dilemma, that is to what extent can each individual's causes, interests, and qualities run parallel with the interests, objectives, and characteristics of a work organization? Furthermore, the vastly increasing number of people with a "flexible" employment contract form an important area for special attention for work and organizational psychology; for example many people do not work "in", but do work "for" a work organization as temps. Another example is the teleworker who communicates with his or her work organization from "a distance". Important issues are, for example, commitment to the organization among stand-by employees, their education and training, social relations among teleworkers, the effectiveness of external ("outsourced") staff positions, etc.

In this sense, the domain of work and organizational psychology can be characterized as the surface of a triangle in which the angular points are formed by the behaviour of (individual) people, their work tasks, and the work organization, and the mutual relations are also paid attention to. Inside this triangle, various emphases in work and organizational psychology may be distinguished. We prefer to speak of distinctions, rather than separate, isolated areas. First and foremost, *work* psychology: in this field topics discussed are for example work and job analysis, task characteristics, determinants of fatigue and mental load, task acceptance and performing task activities, measuring work performance, rest periods and the design of working time arrangements, etc. Attention is generally focused on component characteristics of work tasks, and determinants of the quality of work activities in relation to the capacities and other characteristics of individuals. Second, *personnel* psychology: the topics that are considered to be included are all linked to staff "management" or staff care, for example recruitment, selection and placement, education and training, staff appraisal, development of managers and employees, developing career plans, policy for the elderly, specific measures for minorities, etc. In a certain sense, these topics reflect the "advance" made by an employee from his or her first job up to and including the last job. Third, *organizational* psychology: this encompasses topics such as leadership, decision making, participation and industrial democracy, conflict and power, quality care, (re)design of organizations, organizational culture, and planned processes of change. Important questions are whether such topics exhibit large differences when a distinction is made between profit organizations and non-profit organizations, or between sectors such as industry and commercial service.

Quite many well-known industrial and organizational topics are wanting in the overview provided and we have mentioned only a few examples in passing, in order to make clear the difference in orientation between the three "types" of work and organizational psychology. There is a certain arbitrariness in this trichotomy, however. A topic such as appraisal that has now been mentioned in our discussion of personnel psychology can also be approached from a work psychological point of view, for instance in emphasizing important characteristics of a job that have been identified by means of job analysis. If the question were to be posed to what extent objectives possessing strategic or cultural value for the organization can be realized by means of appraisal, the emphasis is on a more organization psychological perspective. Another example is motivation: it can be approached from any of the three subareas, depending on the problem requiring a solution. What is being stated holds for many more topics; this is why we prefer not to separate these approaches from each another, but to view them in mutual connection as characteristic for work and organizational psychology.

The domain of work and organizational psychology furthermore comprises various *levels of analysis*. As has been noted earlier, the *individual* often forms the level at which analyses of behaviour take place. Consider, for example, the choice of the performance targets that a staff member wishes to accomplish, or the training someone wants to take. Such choices are possibly affected by individual-bound variables such as age, experience, need for achievement, and so on, but probably also by external variables. One might think of the *work task*, for example, of which the duration, degree of difficulty, the skills and capacities required, interruptions (possibly by another task with more urgency), etc. may be the focus of attention. The next level of analysis is the *group*, in which case the central issues are for example the views held by a majority (or by all members together) regarding the quality of the performance to be delivered, the questions how the manager can be influenced best, how a dispute with another department should be dealt with, etc. The behaviour of people at work can none the less also be examined and interpreted at the level of a "business unit" or the entire *organization*. In this case, attention pivots around, for example, the degree to which privatization of a business unit affects people's behaviour (and simultaneously also becomes a success or a failure as a result of that behaviour), around a newly launched system of quality care or the "self-steering" working climate aimed at. Finally, we distinguish the level of the *organizational environment*. Consider the meaning of external "networks" of organizations for the way a company or an institution works, such as an association of branch organizations, an "umbrella" in health care or a conglomerate of banks for an aircraft industry.

In the maiden years of work and organizational psychology—often called industrial psychology at the time—the main emphasis was on the individual. With the development of the discipline, but of course also as a consequence of changing problems in work organizations, the other levels of analysis mentioned gradually emerged more distinctly. In this sense, the history of work and organizational psychology can also be described on the basis of the changes in the level of analysis (see also Chapter 4, this Volume). In this context, what is of particular interest is that data from different levels of analysis, for example those collected within the same study, cannot be related to each other arbitrarily, but often require the use of advanced "multilevel" techniques (see also Chapter 2, this Volume).

WORK AND ORGANIZATIONAL PSYCHOLOGY AS A DISCIPLINE

At all Dutch universities where a full curriculum in psychology may be taken, work and organizational psychology is one of the specializations, though not necessarily under this full name. Smaller or larger groups also exist at the other (technical) universities, which provide courses (in subareas) in work and organizational psychology. In the last 10 to 20 years, the number of students entering was considerable (the reader may find more information on this topic in Chapter 3, this Volume). Similar developments are taking place in many other countries.

Work and organizational psychology did not really "fit" the university curriculum of psychology however, at least not in the well-known typology of the field presented by Duijker (1976). According to Duijker, four types of discipline and an auxiliary science are central to psychology, namely experimental psychology (psychonomics), developmental psychology, personality psychology (individual differences), and behavioural psychology, with methodology as a backing. What is also missing in this typology is social psychology, for example. Duijker however preferred the label "behavioural psychology" and expected that not only the social and cultural conditions of behaviour would be treated via behavioural psychology, but also that the contributions made by the three other disciplines would be integrated.

Is it true, then, that work and organizational psychology—just as other subareas in psychology, such as economic, clinical, and educational psychology—form "applications" of one or several of the disciplinary types just mentioned? It is certainly not. Yet, the perspective of one or several disciplines may be recognized in some work and organizational topics, as may have been made clear by examples provided earlier in this chapter. For example, psychonomics is

recognizable in problems surrounding training and development, design of safer work situations, maximum workload, etc. Developmental psychological topics are to be found in for example management development, socialization of junior employees, and ageing staff members. Personality psychology may be observed in issues such as selection, placement, and appraisal, whereas social-psychological approaches are recognizable in subjects such as semi-autonomous groups, leadership, and conflict behaviour. The importance of methodology is particularly shown in the heavy emphasis on design and methods of research and on data analysis in work and organizational psychology.

The circumstantial fact that a particular discipline (in Duijker's sense)—really an approach starting from one specific *determinant* of behaviour—can be recognized in various work and organizational psychological topics, forms an illustration of the embedding of work and organizational aspects within the whole of psychology. But this fact says little about the immense development that work and organizational psychology as a scientific discipline has shown, both within the university and beyond. Work and organizational psychology would be underrated if it were viewed merely as a "field of application" of other psychological disciplines or subdisciplines; we will return to this topic in the next section. Work and organizational psychology has developed itself as a self-reliant field to a large extent because it has "gone its own way" (see also Chapter 4, this Volume), often in close connection with the "field" of work organizations. Here we will name only a few examples that form a visible piece of evidence, i.e. the theory regarding methods for the appraisal of people would never have developed to such an extent without the empirical and experimental evidence on staff appraisal in organizations. Diagnostics and test research would not have reached their current level without the developments in practice concerning selection and placement. Many theories of motivation and performance models have been sophisticated by being elaborated for work situations, in which specific production targets have to be achieved or performance is realized under pressure. Experiments involving financial reward were based on the question of whether staff members who have specific expectations about consequences of their behaviour at work are high performers. Ergonomics or "human engineering" psychology is a direct result of the need for psychological analyses of work tasks, the optimization of work performance and the reduction of the probability of mistakes, errors, and accidents. Specifically in research on work organizations, theories and insights have developed, or have been refined, in the field of group behaviour, group performance, communication and information, effects of stereotyping, conflict behaviour, resistance to and conditions for change, etc. A great deal of knowledge of stress and strain, and its effects on health and absenteeism from work, has accumulated because of the fact that stressful work was actually included in the research. Obviously, this enumeration is only meant by way of illustration. What we wish to make clear is that work and organizational psychology has gained an independent position at universities, both in the Netherlands and elsewhere, because its reason for existence was clear in the field. Especially because of that interaction between science and practice, many original contributions can be found in work and organizational psychology with regard to theories and models, instruments developed, scientific research, and application of knowledge.

A question that has become increasingly important and may even be crucial for the identity of work and organizational psychology in the years to come (de Wolff & Shimmin, 1994) is the one regarding the relation with other disciplines concerned with work-related and organizational problems. We will approach this relation by adopting two perspectives. Starting from the first perspective, the main emphasis is placed on what distinguishes disciplines: work and organizational sociology is concerned with for example the functioning of societal groupings and with the role played by institutional forces, e.g. concerning differences in access to important resources (knowledge, income, etc.). The focus of work (or micro) economics is on the economic behaviour displayed by employees, managers, or administrators at an aggregated level, for example the extent to which decision making in a company is rational, given uncertain conditions. Technical

business administration concentrates on, for example, the design of production systems and data systems, and therefore also the nature of the "intervention" by people in processes involving production of goods and services. There are still other disciplines and bodies of knowledge operating in the field of work and organization, such as social business administration, political science, human resource science, communication studies, etc. It would extend too far to characterize all these related disciplines separately. Moreover, the "distinctive" perspectives mentioned will not always behave in this precise manner in practice. This is partly the result of actions which involve "moving disciplinary boundaries", performed by those working from a particular discipline. For example, work and organizational psychologists often make productive use of knowledge and insights from sociology and economics, and vice versa. Another part is caused by the fact that usually more similarity appears to exist between theories that have different disciplinary origins than was assumed at first (for instance, economic and psychological models regarding decision making given uncertainty).

A second perspective on the relation with other work and organizational sciences stresses the importance of *multidisciplinarity*. Many topics that work and organizational psychologists find themselves confronted with are not exclusively psychological. Often, however, it is possible to formulate meaningful psychological (aspects of) problems. Theories and research data of other "descent" may also lead to an important broadening of insight. It is our opinion that multidisciplinary frameworks of cooperation should be the rule rather than the exception, both in research and in practice.

The two perspectives mentioned here are not opposed, but form a productive complement. Multidisciplinary approaches are especially realized when the "typical" and characteristic element of conceptualization and approach originating from every involved discipline is emphasized (and therefore also the "limits" of the respective approaches are indicated; Thierry, 1989). It is often in such cases that there is room for and an open view on what other disciplines can contribute. This means, among other things, that attention is paid to an adequate formulation of problems, which brings us to the relationship between pure scientific and applied research in our discipline.

WORK AND ORGANIZATIONAL PSYCHOLOGY: PURE SCIENTIFIC RESEARCH AND APPLIED RESEARCH

In what respects do pure scientific research and applied scientific research differ? In our view, those differences are merely in the *origin of the research problem*. In pure scientific research, the research problem arises in, or in connection with, theoretical questions or previous research; applied research is grounded in problems in practice (see also Chapter 2, this Volume). In applied research, and in industrial and organizational psychology, a practical issue to be resolved therefore plays a role in the foreground or in the background. This immediate "practical relevance" is not the issue in pure scientific research (see also Fagan & Vanden-Bos, 1993).

The distinction between the two types of research is in fact a matter of degree, because, first, results of pure scientific research, in the long term or not, are often highly important for practice (see also Drenth, 1996). Second, research that is set up in connection with a specific problem in a company can produce fundamental insights, generalizable to all kinds of other (work) situations. Depending on the origin of the problem that motivates a study, within work and organizational psychology both types of research therefore occur (see also Roe, 1994). On the other hand, not everyone shares the opinion that pure and applied research differ merely in degree. The view is sometimes found in introductory psychology textbooks that applied psychology (of which, as a rule, work and organizational psychology is generally also thought to be a part) merely applies knowledge from pure research to practice. This is in contrast with Schönpflug (1993) who holds the view that the two types of research cannot be retraced to each other and that they have an entirely different tradition, which may be rooted in ancient Greek philosophy.

Characteristic for much pure scientific research

is the laboratory experiment. Its power lies in its ability to study a single phenomenon under controlled circumstances. Only rarely can these controlled circumstances be found in applied work and organizational psychological research, including the case of a field experiment, because the question from practice with which the researcher is initially confronted is often complex and not always clear (see also Lévy-Leboyer, 1986). This requires the question to be translated into a research problem that is suitable for work and organizational psychological conceptualization and research (and, as has been remarked upon earlier on the subject of multidisciplinarity, if possible also for contributions from other disciplines), in which case a good study of the literature is naturally indispensable. In some cases, results from comparable research are available, on the basis of which relevant hypotheses may be formulated. The literature study may also point out, however, that the research problem is "new" or at least has not been studied in the manner stated, in which case a creative approach is desirable (see also Dunnette, 1990); it is against this background that Lévy-Leboyer (1993) remarks that applied psychology offers a rich source of inventions beyond the scope of the laboratory.

In the following step, the elaboration of the research design, the researcher is confronted with the limitations peculiar to the work organization(s) commissioning or to be studied. To illustrate, if one wishes to study the effect of a novel style of leadership (charismatic, say), one is usually committed to natural, existing groups that are not suitable for "random" allocation of persons across experimental conditions. Furthermore, agreements may have been made beforehand, for example between unions and the company, as to which groups or units will and which ones will not participate in the study. Another issue is that a company or an institution just simply cannot be "brought to a standstill" during a study; all kinds of changes take place during a study that may have a drastic impact on the results of the study at issue. All these "peculiarities" of work and organizational psychological research imply that field experiments often belong to the "quasi-experimental" type, that there are many field studies (surveys) or cases, and that many threats to validity requiring creative solutions occur.

What is, in fact, "applied" in applied (experimental or survey) research? Undoubtedly, the "design" of the study, the specific hypotheses, the instruments, and the methods of data analysis are adjusted ("tailored") to the problem at issue. Such tailored applications also characterize pure scientific research, however. Are the specific recommendations that are made on the basis of the research results also applicatory in nature? This is not so either, really, that is they are "derived" from the results rather than based on application; considering the specific circumstances of this particular company, certain interventions are expected to qualify to a higher extent and other ones probably to a lesser extent. Such derived recommendations also occur when a work and organizational psychologist is asked the question to contribute to the solution of a problem on the basis of his or her scientific knowledge, without there being any room for separate empirical research.

Hence we see that the concept of "applied" hardly has a clarifying effect when it comes to characterizing work and organizational psychology in terms of its relation with other psychological subdisciplines. We tend to speak of application in handling an instrument (for example a test or a scale) that has been developed for general use, in a particular specified case (for example assessing job satisfaction of staff members within a company). Another well-known situation is the one in which the work and organizational psychologist uses his or her knowledge to give individual clients advice (for example in selecting a career), or becomes involved in implementing advice given. Importantly, this does require doing the advising and acting in accordance with the universal scientific maxims (precision and objectivity of observation, verification of assumptions, avoidance of unwarranted claims, and so on). A totally different type of situation is the case in which the work and organizational psychologist is actually asked to use his or her knowledge in decisions, actions, or interventions. In this case, we speak of use or exploitation of psychological research and psychological insights. The primary criterion is no longer whether something is (scientifically) correct, but rather whether it works, or whether it is useful and effective.

FUTURE TOPICS FOR WORK AND ORGANIZATIONAL PSYCHOLOGY

When we, the editors, were engaged in specifying the content of this new *Handbook* some years ago, we expected that an "update" would suffice for various chapters from the first *Handbook*. We now believe we were in error on that score. All these chapters have therefore been drastically revised and largely rewritten, but without many changes to the titles of these chapters, however. In this way we wish to express our expectation that many changes and innovations will take place in the field of the regular, often classic, topics in work and organizational psychology. Of course, drastic changes also take place in work organizations apart from "this month's fad", for example in computerization and work, in the globalization of markets, and in the increasingly self-steering character of organization units. For the greater part, however, the major changes thus occurring in the "working people–work tasks–work organization" triangle are related to the topics that have been included in this new *Handbook* (and for example in the *Handbook* edited by Dunnette and Hough (1990–94)). The same conclusion can be drawn if special attention is paid to possible consequences of new insights in other fields of psychology. For the very same reason, Cascio (1995) formulates his research agenda for the 21st century in terms of classic topics such as job analysis, selection, training and development, performance appraisal, performance-dependent reward, and organization development.

In addition, we also expect some new, or restated, topics. Most of these have to do with the circumstantial fact that work organizations are becoming increasingly less hierarchical, that very often business units and work tasks are altered drastically, that more temporary contracts will apply to people, that working hours and workdays will exhibit a great deal of variety, that (groups of) employees will become more self-reliant (Frese,

1996), and that conditions of employment and social security will be individualized to a greater extent. We will briefly touch on some topics:

- Because workers will have to attend to all kinds of matters themselves to a greater extent, much research will concern concepts such as self-efficacy, self-identity, self-control, self-esteem, self-monitoring, self-learning, etc.
- How are more "self-steering" people motivated in their work? By what variables is effective and productive behaviour at work influenced? What is the role played by commitment and involvement? etc.
- What is understood by quality of work? How can health at work be promoted? Can causes of stress be reduced?
- How will organizations undergo planned radical changes when most of their members "direct" themselves?
- What will be the effect of certain stable and fundamental personality characteristics in relation to or in interaction with (rapidly) changing characteristics of work (see for instance Nicholson, 1996)?
- Finally, a fundamental and increasingly important topic for future society: To what extent can we suffice with (the application of) general insights and regularities, or should we aim for a much more differentiated "contingent" approach instead, in which cultural and ethnic differences and differences in values and convictions held by people are taken into consideration to a greater extent than before?

THE ORGANIZATION OF THIS HANDBOOK

The following chapters of this first volume are concerned with definitional, historical, and methodological fundamentals. They explore the nature of the studies in work and organizational psychology, the role played by the (professional) work and organizational psychologist, and the way in which work and organizational psychology has developed in Europe.

The three subsequent volumes generally follow the perspective of different levels of analysis referred to earlier in this chapter. Volume 2, "Work Psychology", concentrates on the issues related to the direct relationship between the worker/employer and his or her task or function. The third volume on "Personnel Psychology" deals with many classical subjects from personnel management or, as it is generally termed nowadays, human resource management. Volume 4 focuses on the organization as a system, in which both organizational processes and the organization–environment interaction are discussed.

Every classification has some artificiality and arbitrariness about it. Some chapters could be justifiably categorized in another Volume. But an attempt has been made to discuss the whole spectrum of issues from work and organizational psychology in an increasingly wider context starting with the micro level of the person–task interaction and concluding with the discussion of the organization in relation to its environment.

REFERENCES

Cascio, W.F. (1995). Whither industrial and organizational psychology in a changing world of work? *American Psychologist, 50*, 928–939.

Drenth, P.J.D. (1996). Psychology as a science: Truthful or useful? *European Psychologist, 1*, 3–13.

Duijker, H.C.J. (1976). De psychologie en de psychologiein. *Nederlands Tijdschrift voor de Psychologie, 31*, 503–511.

Dunnette, M.D. (1990). Blending the science and practice of industrial and organizational psychology: Where are we and where are we going? In M.D. Dunnette & L.M. Hough (Eds.), *Handbook of industrial and organizational psychology* (2nd ed, Vol. 1). Palo Alto, CA: Consulting Psychologists Press.

Dunnette, M.D., & Hough, L.M. (Eds.). (1990–94). *Handbook of industrial and organizational psychology* (2nd ed, Vols. 1–4). Palo Alto, CA: Consulting Psychologists Press.

Fagan, T.K., & VandenBos, G.R. (Eds.). (1993). *Exploring applied psychology: Origins and critical analyses.* Washington DC: American Psychological Association.

Frese, M. (1996). *Preparing work and organizational psychology for the 21st century: Self-reliance at work.* Amsterdam: University of Amsterdam.

Lévy-Leboyer, C. (1986). Applying psychology or

applied psychology? In F. Heller (Ed.), *The use and abuse of social science.* London: Sage.

Lévy-Leboyer, C. (1993). The chicken and the egg: Which came first? *Applied Psychology: An International Review, 42,* 52–54.

Nicholson, N. (1996). Towards a new agenda for work and personality: Traits, self-identity, "strong" interactionism, and change. *Applied Psychology: An International Review, 45,* 189–205.

Roe, R.A. (1994). *Work and organizational psychology as a basic discipline: An alternative view and its implications.* Paper presented at the Third Symposium on Organizational Behavior, Lisbon, June.

Schönpflug, W. (1993). Applied psychology: Newcomer with a long tradition. *Applied Psychology: An International Review, 42,* 5–30.

Thierry, H. (1989). Imperialisme of contingentie. Een blik vanuit de arbeidsen organisatiepsychologie. [Imperialism or contingency: A view from industrial and organizational psychology]. In H. Thierry & A. Evers (Eds.), *Psychologie en Hoger Onderwijs: Toekomstverkenningen.* Lisse, Netherlands: Swets & Zeitlinger.

Wolff, C.J. de, & Shimmin, S. (1994). Complexities and choices: Work psychology in Europe. *European Work and Organizational Psychologist, 4, 333–341.*

2

Research in Work and Organizational Psychology: Principles and Methods

Pieter J.D. Drenth

1 INTRODUCTION

This chapter provides an overview of the research methods used in work and organizational psychology. Naturally, one should not expect an exhaustive review of the abundance of methods applied in this field in such a limited space. Nor does this chapter include a manual for designing research in the field of work and organizational (hereafter W&O) psychology. For a discussion of more technical aspects, such as the appropriate design and phasing of a research project, sampling, the construction and testing of instruments, and statistically accounting for interpretations, one is referred to the relevant literature (Hays, 1963; Nunnally; 1967; Runkel & McGrath, 1972; Weiss, 1976; Babbie, 1979; Meerling, 1980; Ghiselli et al., 1981; Bobko, 1990; Drenth & Sijtsma, 1990; Sackett & Larson, 1990; Keppel, 1991; Rosenthal & Rosnov, 1991; Breakwell et

al., 1995). This chapter focuses on discussing the principles and assumptions inherent in the research process in this area of psychology.

Why, one might wonder, would one devote a rather extensive chapter in a handbook in an applied field such as W&O psychology to scientific research and its methods? Has not enough research been done and enough understanding gained to shift the emphasis toward the application of this understanding instead of doing even more research? And, considering the large number of students attracted to more applied areas, isn't the interest in and the direct involvement in scientific research among W&O psychologists declining? Furthermore, when it comes to tackling problems in practice, isn't the focus on a certain approach, instilling of certain attitudes and stimulating problem-solving processes rather than on generating or using scientific knowledge?

A first reaction to these questions is that, just as many of the indispensable current insights in W&O psychology are based on past research, scientific research will remain essential for the development of future understanding. Many questions have not fully been answered (as yet) and many others have not been studied at all. Furthermore, through social, technological, and organizational developments, new problems which need to be solved arise almost daily. Think of, for instance, the effects and requirements of new technologies and computerization. In other words, the process of developing W&O psychological knowledge is far from over, and many insights based on past research become outdated through new developments. Finally, a characteristic feature of research-based knowledge is that on the one hand it provides useful and reliable laws and principles, but on the other hand the validity of these relations and principles is often limited by restrictions in research conditions, samples or circumstances. Therefore, continuing research is the best way to guarantee advancing insight, also in applied scientific fields.

In addition, knowledge of scientific research methods is also of great importance to practitioners for other reasons. Even though many of these practitioners are not actively involved in research themselves, in their approach to and solution of many problems they will either have to fall back on earlier research or come to the conclusion that further research is necessary. To understand and critically evaluate such research, knowledge of the principles of research is a *sine qua non*. This applies even more when the assistance of an external research agency or institute is enlisted to carry out such research. Knowledge of research methodology will then be indispensable in order to be able to critically evaluate conclusions, weigh proposals, and to derive the proper implementations.

In this chapter we shall successively discuss: the characteristics of a scientific approach, the different types of research that can be found in W&O psychology, the relationship between science and application, a number of specific research problems, and the different types of research designs found in W&O psychology. An overview of the methods of data collection in W&O psychology will conclude this chapter.

2 CHARACTERISTICS OF A SCIENTIFIC LINE OF THOUGHT

As was stated earlier the scientific line of thought is characterized by a number of typical features distinguishing it from non-scientific knowledge, which is based on experience, common sense and anecdotal data. Naturally, the latter type of knowledge is largely truthful and useful and to disregard it as meritless would be a sign of arrogance. However, scientific knowledge is characterized by several elements that give this kind of knowledge an advantage and a surplus value. Scientific methods of knowledge acquisition have a better chance of resulting in accurate insight in the phenomena of interest. Moreover, those insights not only relate to existing phenomena and their interrelations but also to future developments. The latter opens the door to making predictions and taking precautionary or adaptive measures.

Which are those elements characterizing the process of scientific knowledge acquisition?

First, the unbiased way of posing a question and searching for an answer. Designing research in a scientific manner demands honest and unbiased planning, in which both data supporting a certain theory or hypothesis as well as data leading to the rejection of this theory or hypothesis are given an equal chance. In other words, one does not only search for data corroborating a theory or hypothesis, but just as much—or according to Popper (1959) especially—for data which could falsify these.

A second characteristic is, that in some way or another, (*research*) *data* are collected that are supposed to lead the aforementioned support or weakening of theoretical assumptions. The word "data" does not only refer to the so-called "hard facts". As will become clear in the course of this chapter, the nature of data can vary from subjective judgements or opinions (results from questionnaires, interviews or observations) to highly objective facts (the number of days of absence, the number of rejected products, volume of turnover). The precision of the data varies with their nature; however this must be weighed against their relevance and the generalizability of the interpretations. In any case, conclusions drawn from scientific research should, whenever possible, be based on relevant data. As such psychology, and obviously also W&O psychology, is an empirical science.

Next, these data are *collected* in a systematic manner. Terms such as standardization and objectivity pertain to this process. Standardization entails a maximal control over the circumstances which could influence the perceived phenomenon. If one wants to study the impact of music on work, one must be sure that the conditions for the experimental group working with music and for the control group working without music are as similar as possible in order to be able to attribute found differences in performance or experiences to the factor "music". Proper standardization will not always be possible. When the observations are less standardized the varying circumstances will have to be recorded as detailed as possible, in order to be able to indicate limitations of the conclusions and to generate alternative explanations for the differences found.

Objectivity refers to the degree to which different observers or judges are able to record the data in the same manner. Judgement or classification of data in scientific research should not be substantially influenced by the subjectivity of the observer. This is not to say that it is possible or even necessary to fully eliminate the subjectivity of the observer. In a certain sense, any observation or judgement is, being a psychological process, subjective. Moreover, it seems wise to take Köbben's (1991) warning into account, depicting a threatening image of the researcher (interviewer, observer) as a robot-like, depersonalized office clerk. However, through standardization and systematization of the procedure, this subjective process can lead to a result which would also be reached by other expert observers or judges; a (certain) objectivity in the sense of inter-subjectivity. Even in cases in which data collection is too strongly linked to the person of the researcher ("engaged" interviewers, participating observers) it is still possible to reach most of this ideal through self-discipline and conscientiousness. Intensive preparation, elaborate recording of data, consistency throughout the interview and trying to

find data that corroborate other data from the interview as well as "circumstantial evidence", should enlarge the objectivity.

To measure agreement one needs at least two independent judges. How the measurement of agreement is calculated, depends mostly upon two factors (Zeegers, 1989). In the first place, the level of measurement of the data is important. Data can be qualitative, that is, judges categorize persons or objects. Data can also be quantitative, that is, on an ordinal or interval level. In the second place, it depends on the extent to which the judge's scores must be taken "seriously". For instance, it is possible that a consistent difference in mean scores of two judges does not reflect "a lack of agreement", but is caused by the tendency of one of the judges to systematically give higher scores than the other. Such a tendency is a characteristic of the judge (benevolence, leniency) rather than an indication of a lack of agreement about the judged people.

The choice of a measure of agreement also depends on the number of judges (two or more than two), and on whether agreement should be determined for a number of objects or people or for a single object or person. Well-known measures of agreement include Cohen's kappa for qualitative data (Cohen, 1960) and the product-moment correlation coefficient. The latter measure is obviously meant to assess the agreement between two judges with regard to quantitative data. For an overview of agreement measures for two judges one is referred to Zeegers (1989) and for more than two judges to Shrout and Fleiss (1979), Tinsley and Weiss (1975) or Lawlis and Lu (1972). Popping (1983) provides an overview of measures for qualitative data.

A fourth characteristic of the scientific line of thinking is that the analysis and interpretation of data should be conducted as unbiased as possible. This implies, in the first place, that all available data should be used; no selection or prioritizing of data, influenced by prior expectations, hopes or fears should be allowed.

Next, the process of analysis and interpretation itself should be neutral and impartial. No ideology, authority or interest group should be allowed to influence scientific reasoning and argumentation *per se*. There can be no room for ideologies, world views, political objectives or religious convictions, just as there can be no room for prejudices, wishful thinking or twaddle. In this sense, science is value-free, subject only to analytical, logical norm (Drenth, 1994). At the same time, this requirement implies that statements, expectations and hypotheses should be formulated in such a way that they can be tested against the facts, not only by the researcher but also by others. This leads to the requirements of testability, explicability and replicability; three important criteria for the scientific character of research.

The fact that ideologies and interests are not supposed to influence the scientific process of interpretation also implies that power should never play a role in scientific debates. Only reasonable and rational arguments should exert influence. Power pressure is alien to the process of scientific reasoning and only the non-power or persuasive relationship is acceptable (Mulder, 1977). De Groot (1971) has even defended that in science debates in fact only the principle of consensus should be acceptable and that the democratic majority model, which is valid for questions where answers imply more than logical and empirical arguments, does not apply here.

Naturally, the aforementioned does not imply that power (positions) do(es) not play a part in the daily practice of scientific research. Unfortunately, it is hard to deny that non-scientific factors, among which power related ones, are of importance in the discussions on "schools" and methods, the acceptance of articles, the allocation of funds, and the results of (often applied) scientific research.

A final characteristic of scientific research concerns a combination of seemingly opposing factors. First, being "open" to new developments, providing new initiatives with the benefit of the doubt they deserve and presenting room for creative ideas. This pertains to content (new theories, new explanations, Kühn, 1962) as well as method and approach (Phillips, 1973). Rigidity would prove disastrous for both these aspects of scientific activity. On the other hand one must also realize that science is both *communicative* and *cumulative*. That is, new ideas, new approaches and new paradigms need to be tested through open communication with fellow researchers (De

Groot's "forum" (1990)), or even with any reasonable other (Hofstee's "universal public" (1975)). They should also be evaluated in light of the existing knowledge and insights. In other words, not every innovation is valid and certainly not for its own sake. Scientific activity is an activity in the area of tension between creativity and testing, or the area of tension between openness and continuity (Van Strien, 1978).

The above dealt with several ideal criteria for scientific research. Not all work that is done by scientists meets these standards. Also, the label "scientific" used by persons or institutions does not guarantee the scientific character in the sense described above. One should continuously and critically judge the merits of proclaimed scientific research by the aforementioned criteria. Ultimately, this is only possible when the requirement of openness, of publicity, or as Hofstee (1975) phrased it "the postulate of vulnerability", is met. That is why this last requirement may be regarded as pivotal for the practice of science.

3 TYPES OF RESEARCH

In the preceding section an overview of the essential characteristics of scientific research was presented. Naturally, the form and the process that different research projects take are not uniform. Reality, including the reality of scientific research, is immensely varied. In the following section we will elucidate the different types of research common to the field of W&O psychology. The first type of research we will describe is aimed at the "instruments" used for collecting data: instrumental research. Next, we will distinguish four types of research aimed at the four goals of empirical research: description, exploration, explanation, and interpretation.

3.1 Instrumental research
As mentioned before, the first type of research is aimed at constructing and calibrating instruments, which are often to be applied in many other research contexts, or in the context of diagnostics or (personnel) decision making. One could think of the construction of psychological tests,

appraisal systems, interview schemes, scales for self-rating, satisfaction scales and suchlike.

The analysis and evaluation of the psychological significance of that which is operationalized in the test or scale, constitute the scientific character of this kind of research. The construction of an instrument in itself does not yet make for scientific research, even when done entirely in accordance with the rules of the art of construction. Only through evaluation of the psychological meaning of the instrument, preferably in terms of a psychological theory, does this construction become more than a technology. Examples of instrumental research in the field of W&O psychology are: the development of tests for personnel selection (Herriot, 1989), of scales measuring job satisfaction (Job Description Index; Smith, Kendall, & Hulin, 1969, see also Biessen, 1992), of questionnaires judging leadership qualities (Bass, 1990), and of instruments for the measurement of all kinds of organizational characteristics (Pugh et al., 1968; Price, 1972; Cozijnsen & Vrakking, 1993; Sims et al., 1993).

3.2 Descriptive research

This type of research is aimed at systematically identifying and recording a certain phenomenon, process, collection or system. Although different dimensions or possible determinants may play a part in this description, the main goal is the analysis of a phenomenon, individual, group or population (restricted by time and to a particular area). Important is that this type of research is not directly or indirectly aimed at testing an expectation, hypothesis or theory but is merely directed at systematically recording the object of study. Admittedly, however, this recording is always done from a certain perspective or point of view.

Different types of research are included in this category. Obviously the first is the systematic categorization of phenomena, events or processes within a certain domain such as the European science and technology (European Commission, 1994), or tests and test research in The Netherlands (Evers, Van Vliet-Mulder & Ter Laak, 1992).

In the second place, the "case study" which entails the systematic description of a single case: descriptions of organizational change or develop-

ment (see cases in Luthans, 1992) or of decision making processes (Koopman et al., 1981) are good examples. Also, the systematic uncovering of thought or cognitive analyses, for example, through protocol analysis, aims to obtain a description of information processing, choices and decisions which is as complete and rich as possible. This type of research is in some ways related to theory-oriented research which will be described hereafter. Through case studies one tries either to find new theoretical interpretations or to gain more in-depth knowledge pertaining to existing theoretical insights.

Thirdly, the measurement and summary in a descriptive format (numerical or verbal) of different facets of an entire population, such as a characterization of workers in a certain organization, a school population or the members of a club. The aim can also be an approach of the aforementioned analysis of the population, through studying a sample of the latter. In this case, the characterization of the entire population is provided through statistical inferences from the results found for the sample. One of the first large-scale W&O psychological studies in the Netherlands (COP, 1959), which pertained to first first line supervisors in industry, can serve as an example here.

3.3 Explorative research

This type of research shares with the next type of research that will be described (explanatory research) the fact that it is "theory-oriented". All research in W&O psychology in which empirical data are collected and interpreted without aiming at insight in a specific sample (or population from which this sample is drawn) or instrument, falls within these two categories. Data are used to explore or test certain theoretical relationships.

The term "theory" does not always have to be interpreted pretentiously in this context. In a theoretical explanation the aim is to establish relations between actual observations through deploying certain conceptual systems, or as Runkel and McGrath put it simply: "Theory is a guide to tell you where to look for what you want to observe" (1972, p.23).

As on the one hand observation and exploration will never be fully "theory-free" and on the other hand empirical or experimental validation in the social and behavioural sciences will never be "foolproof", it would be better to think in terms of a fluent line running from exploration to explanation. Whether a study should be located closer to the one or to the other extreme depends on the degree to which one has been able to explicitly formulate a theory or, more specifically, a set of hypotheses.

On the one hand, there is the hypotheses-generating or *explorative* research. This type of research is aimed at generating hypothetical explanations of phenomena. By "exploring" cues and indications in the empirical material in an objective (using, for example, factor or cluster analysis) or subjective way (by, for example, making an inventory of expert opinions) one tries to discover possible relationships, possible interactions, and possible causal relations. Explorative research should always be followed by attempts to test the hypotheses. Thus, this type of research is often the first stage of a larger research project.

There are two circumstances which call for explorative research. The first is a situation in which the researcher is unable to formulate clear hypotheses or expectations on basis of his own or others' experience or on basis of existing theories. The second is a situation in which the field of research turns out to be so complicated and many of the variables in the study are so difficult to control that the empirical relations found would not amount to more than hypothetical explanations anyhow. These relations then need to be tested in a more controlled setting or through a more focused research question.

As said before, it is questionable whether clear examples of "theory-free" explorative research are available. Often, (implicit) theories will have played a part in the choice of relations to be explored as well as in the choice of variables taken into account.

A possible misunderstanding has to be warned against: a large-scale research project is often proceeded by a so called "pilot" study. This is often described in terms of the "exploratory or explorative phase". However, when the goal of this pilot study amounts to no more than testing the value of the concepts used or the usefulness of a questionnaire etc. (which is often the goal of the

pilot phase), then the use of term "explorative research" is less appropriate. After all, this is not a matter of generating hypotheses or expectations.

3.4   Explanatory research

Hypotheses-testing research or explanatory research can be placed at the other extreme of the continuum. This type of research may entail a large variety of problems, such as answering the question why people or groups behave in a certain way, why certain organizations are effective, growing or flexible and others are not, why certain (un)desirable effects occur under certain conditions etc. Explanations which, in essence, always have a deductive-nomological form: for a category of phenomena a general statement holds (all human beings are mortal), a concrete case is part of this category (Socrates is a human being), thus the conclusion (Socrates is mortal) can be logically inferred.

In the social and behavioural sciences, these conclusions usually have a probabilistic rather than an absolute nature. The conclusion then contains restricted additions such as: in most cases, greater chance, significantly more, etc. This has several causes. In the first place, the general statement in the deductive-nomological model is usually based on a probabilistic relation: "Most candidates with an IQ above 120 will pass the computer programming exam" or "Where motivation of pupils is too strong, often their performance will again start declining". In the second place, the methods and instruments in these disciplines are far from being perfectly reliable. This implies that assigning an actual case (person, phenomenon) to a category (candidates with IQ scores above 120, strongly motivated pupils) also has a probabilistic character. Thirdly, all experimental testing is embedded in a system of arrangements and traditions regarding, for instance, sample size, levels of significance and suchlike.

A special, and for W&O psychology interesting, category of explanatory research is the so-called *causal explanatory* research: testing which events or facts lead to, or cause, other facts or events.

In this case, the general term of the earlier mentioned syllogism has a causal explanatory character: high levels of job satisfaction lead to low absence; participation in decision making leads to the acceptance of leaders ... Whether the cause described in the general statement is actually responsible for the observed phenomenon (low absenteeism, acceptance of the leader) again depends on two conditions. First, the validity of the general causal statement, keeping in mind as explained above, explanatory statements are mainly probabilistic in character. Secondly, the degree to which alternative explanations (low absenteeism due to the threat of being fired, acceptance of the leader due to his granting of large rewards) can be excluded.

At this moment, scientific research in W&O psychology is primarily aimed at generating and corroborating the general statements described earlier; preferably the general causal statements as these have a stronger explanatory character. As said before, most of these statements have, and will remain to have, a probabilistic rather than a deterministic character. This should not be defended through the meta-physical argument that human freedom and autonomy make deterministic explanations impossible on principle. We would rather uphold the position that, within a causal deterministic model, social and psychological phenomena are determined by multiple causes, and we are almost never able to determine a complete picture of the abundance of causal factors. At the same time, the researcher's challenge is to attempt to keep on adding new understanding and evidence to the already existing insight through finding and determining additional causal relationships and explanatory factors.

Causal research always starts with devising and formulating a hypothetical explanation for a phenomenon observed. This hypothetical explanation can be inspired by existing theories or past research. It could also result from new, creative theoretical ideas. In a next step, the hypothetical explanations must be tested using (new) empirical material.

Hamakers (1990) describes three preconditions for the determination of causal relationships. The first entails an observed relationship in the expected direction. Secondly, there should be sound arguments for the assumption that the causal relationship runs from the alleged cause to the alleged outcome and not vice versa. Thirdly,

the absence of interfering factors, which could cause non-existent causal relationships "to be observed" or existent causal relationships not to be observed, should be ensured.

Clearly, establishing relationships, for instance, finding significant correlations, is a necessary but not a sufficient precondition for determining cause-outcome relationships. Later in this chapter we will cover this important aspect of scientific research in W&O psychology, the causal relationship, in more detail.

As stated, between the extremes of purely explorative and purely explanatory research a large research area is found, which can neither be classified as typically explorative nor as typically explanatory; often uniting characteristics of both types of research. Many large-scale field studies could serve as examples here; for instance, the research into the influence of the nature of decisions on the relationship between participation and effectiveness of decisions (Heller et al., 1988), or the research into the influence of legislative measures on actual involvement of employees in decision making in organizations (IDE, 1981a, 1993). The choice of variables or relationships that were studied in this kind of research were not chosen entirely without theoretical background or without tenable expectations. Therefore, these studies are not merely meant to generate hypotheses. However, they are not purely designed to test hypotheses either. In such studies explicitly formulated hypotheses are too often missing. Also, even outcomes that contradict the expectations are not always that surprising, or can be made plausible by drawing attention to uncontrolled or situation-specific "contingencies".

However, the acknowledgement of this "blending" of explorative and explanatory research should not lead to expectations too readily to being regarded as theories and hypotheses as proven explanations. Neither should this lead to a situation in which, due to negligence or intellectual laziness, one refrains from formulating hypotheses or expectations before collecting or at least before the first analyses of the data. It does imply, however, that the abundance of thorough and careful analyses of the often complex empirical material which can be found in the field of W&O psychology, cannot be classified as either fully fledged hypothesis testing research or as extensive explorative research.

3.5   Interpretative research

A last type of research is not in fact empirical in nature, that is, it is not aimed at or dependent on testing against empirical data. The issue here is interpretation, fitting experiences or findings in a theoretical framework. Due to the rarity or exceptionality of the object of analysis, an empirical test of the interpretation is not possible.

In a broader perspective one could think of a historical or cultural explanation of, for instance, national or international processes (Huizinga, 1986). Another example would be providing a plausible explanation for developments in movements or organizations from a certain social-historical or political perspective (IDE, 1981b).

According to certain authors, intentional explanation (Elster, 1983) or hermeneutic interpretation (De Boer, 1980) is indeed essential for understanding human behaviour, and thus for the methodology of psychology. Only in a true dialogue between responsible and accountable people will this intentionality of human kind surface, according to De Boer (1980). The ethnomethodological trend in sociology (see Handel, 1982) also tries to understand people's intentions in their specific context and their individuality.

It cannot be denied that such intentional interpretation of an experience, a dialogue, a dream or a projective test performance can lead to interesting and surprising understanding of human motives. However, it is clear that the poor testability and the unverifiability of these types of interpretations are their major Achilles' heel, and that the boundary between insightful interpretation and unjustifiable speculation is not always clear and will often be crossed. De Groot (1961, 9.2) presents several directives and restrictions for the methodology of interpretation. It will be clear that the line between descriptive and interpretative research is often thin, as much descriptive research and many case study analyses are also aimed at increasing "clarity" and "understanding" of certain individual cases or processes.

The development of and research on *models* for certain behavioural systems have a distinct position in this area. Such models are ontological, as

opposed to being heuristic. A model is *heuristic* when the different categories of variables that are part of the study are grouped according to their (presumed) mutual relationships. This is done for instance, to check for completeness or also to use as a guideline in formulating possible hypotheses about correlations and cause-effect relationships.

The *ontological* model is designed to simulate reality as closely as possible. The analysis of the model will then also provide insight in reality. Nowadays, ontological models are often simulated with the aid of computers. The advantage of such a computer model is that it allows for studying extreme events which hardly ever occur in reality, or for analysing the consequences of certain influences that are not testable in practice due to the high costs or risks involved. Examples of topics studied in this way are safety behaviour (Wagenaar, Volume 2, Chapter 4 in this Handbook) and consumer decision-making processes or market behaviour (see e.g. Engel et al., 1968).

4   SCIENCE AND APPLICATION

In this section the relationship between scientific research and its practical application will be discussed. It is often asserted that the more field-oriented areas of psychology (clinical, educational and also W&O psychology) can in fact only be characterized as applied sciences. At the same time it is also interesting to see how this applied research, then, relates to policy and action, especially from the perspective of so-called "action-research". For further clarification it seems useful to make several distinctions with regard to the perspectives from which scientific research is undertaken, and then to see where W&O psychology stands in these matters.

In the first place a distinction can be made between *applied research* and *pure scientific research*. The crucial question here is: what motivated the research and what was the origin of the research problem? If the research question originates in a practical question, difficulty or dilemma, if in other words, it is "field induced", then we are dealing with applied research. However, if the issue examined by the researcher, was prompted by scientific curiosity, or through questions raised in previous research because of incomplete or incorrect theoretical explanation, then we speak of pure scientific research.

Applied and purely scientific research do not only differ on the origination of their research questions, they also have different *goals and orientations*. On the one hand the focus can be on decisions or goals that are not inherent in scientific research itself: policy measures, decisions or applications of technology. On the other hand there is free scientific research. Here the objective is to acquire insight and not to see whether it has any practical usefulness or yields applicable results. This dual purpose leads to the distinction between "decision versus conclusion oriented research" (Cronbach & Suppes, 1969).

Formally speaking, there is no difference between applied and pure scientific research. The same scientific rules and norms apply in both types of research. Both types of research lead to generalizable insights and laws. The difference concerns only the origin of the research question and the aim of the research. Is it meant to contribute to a theoretical framework, or is it meant to offer a helping hand in the solution of a practical problem?

Although the majority of the research work carried out in W&O psychology is of an applied character, the literature in this field provides plenty of examples of pure research. Research work on personality (Maslow, 1954), achievement motivation (McClelland, 1961), evaluation and appraisal processes (Frank & Hackman, 1975; Schmidt, 1976), decision making (Heller et al., 1988), group processes (Janis, 1982) or cross-cultural comparisons of organizational behaviour (Hofstede, 1980) are just a few illustrative cases in point.

On the other hand, it will be clear that the majority of research in W&O psychology has an applied character. Most of the research in the well-known areas of testing and selection, training, performance appraisal, ergonomics, worker motivation, leadership, inter-group relations, safety and accidents, organizational processes, decision-making, consumer behaviour and the like is either initiated by practical problems or requests, or leads to practical decisions, procedural advice or applicable instruments, or both.

When regarded more closely it becomes that the distinction made here does not constitute a 100% pure discriminant function. First of all, there is much research, especially in W&O psychology with a twofold intention, aimed at both acquiring theoretical insight and solving a practical problem. It has also repeatedly been found that purely scientific research induces highly varied and useful applications. The application may not have been the primary intention; it is, however, the *de facto* implication. An example of this process is the stimulating effect of theoretical personality research on the development of tests and rating scales. On the other hand it is also often found that primarily applied research leads to important breakthroughs in theoretical understanding. Research in the field of ergonomics and the analysis of processes used in employee appraisal are examples of this type of research.

Secondly, there are also intermediate forms of research, for instance described in the OECD Frascati manual as "fundamental strategical research". This term refers to research at the meeting point of supply (universities, research institutes) and demand (society, industry). Strategic research is oriented towards application, but has such a fundamental character that it furthers science as such at the same time. It is research which takes place within a long-term programme, even if it deals with urgent societal problems. A good deal of the more fundamental research in W&O psychology belongs in this category.

It will have struck the reader that I have not used or referred to concepts such as "fundamental" of "basic" research in the foregoing discussion. The reason for this is that these concepts are not appropriate to our distinction. Of course, basic research, defined as research aimed at the clarification of basic principles in a certain scientific area, and certainly fundamental research, which focuses on the very fundamental questions of the nature and inner dynamics of a scientific phenomenon under study, often have a "purely scientific research" character, but are not identical to the latter. Much "basic" research has an "applied" character, and much applied research turns out to make a genuinely fundamental contribution to the discipline.

One other problem pertaining to this discussion deserves our attention. Is the systematic study of a patient or a job applicant, or of a given organization or man-machine system also scientific research? And, if so, how does it fit into the classification as described above?

In our opinion the criterion for research to be scientific remains whether it leads to generalizable laws and relationships. Occasionally, studies of individual cases may be directed at such general principles (as is the case, for instance, in exemplary case studies, in-depth analyses of individuals aiming at the generation of hypotheses, or the validation of specific interpretations). But this is not usually the case; the intention is usually to gain insight into a single individual (in order to advise, help or cure that individual) or a single system (in order to change or improve that system), making conscientious and critical use of existing scientific knowledge. This is no longer scientific research, but rather its *application* in particular, individual cases.

It is important to realize that veracity is still a valid criterion for this category. One still adheres to the norms and rules of the "scientific game" such as accuracy, the need for precision of observation, the avoidance of gratuitous statements, and the requirement to verify the surmised. One is still seeking for correct understanding and truthful knowledge, but the objective is no longer a generalizable insight into human behaviour.

Sometimes, however, the dividing line between this and the previous category becomes indistinct. The experience of a proficient organizational adviser, the "stored information" of an experienced selection psychologist, or the "tacit knowledge" of a competent therapist may approach the general laws of understanding generated by scientific research. And if these experienced practitioners take the trouble to write up their accumulated insights this often represents an enrichment of the existing scientific literature, as has been demonstrated by organizational scientists like Drucker, Morgan and Kets de Vries.

There is one other aspect of this type of understanding of an individual case which should be mentioned, and this is one which may carry it

beyond the status of "application of science". Most individual cases do not fit exactly into the categories that have been developed in scientific research and to which the validated laws and relationships apply. The problems with which they are faced are often difficult to define, and fixed solutions do not usually apply. Many organizational situations are uncertain, complex, unstable and have to be contextualized in order to be understood. In a sense they are frequently unique. A skilled professional does more than merely apply, in each individual situation, that which is known to hold for a category of cases or organization to which the case in question belongs. In trying to fully understand the individual phenomenon or person he/she uses general scientific insights, but also wisdom and experience; he/she tries to place the case in the context of the specific environment and time, and he/she may even develop (and test!) new theories for that individual case. In other words, professional activity goes beyond what Schön (1987) calls (and rejects as) "technical rationality", and develops into an intellectual process which Peterson (1995) describes as "reflection-in-action".

In my view there are no grounds for demeaning this practice from an arrogant scientific perspective, but we must guard against the temptation to drift off into an "intuitive never-never land" (Peterson, 1995). Accepting veracity as an important criterion means adhering to the scientific rules that were described above. Wherever possible, independent validating indicators and supporting information should be sought and hypotheses and assumptions should be subjected to systematic scientific scrutiny.

A principally different situation is presented when scientific research and its results are utilized to benefit decisions actions or interventions. We then enter the field of *using* science.

The criterion is no longer scientific veracity, but a value-based outcome, such as greater economic growth, a more effective change process, a higher degree of well-being among the workforce, an improved corporate image, and the like. In this vein it can be said that organizational developers, personnel selection psychologists, management developers and trainers (like psychotherapists and pedagogues) are, in this capacity, not scientists but social practitioners. Personal, social or economic norms and values ultimately determine the decisions arrived at and the actions taken. The critical question is no longer: *Is it true*? but: *Does it work*?

We just made a clear distinction between knowledge (veracity) and use (efficacy). A term expressing a line of thinking in social and behavioural sciences that hopes to bridge the gap between scientific research and practical decision making is "action research", first introduced by Kurt Lewin (1946). The term refers to an approach in which the researcher actively brings about change in a social system, intending to change the system (use of knowledge) and to generate critical knowledge about it (creation of knowledge) (Susman & Evered, 1978). Let us examine briefly to what extent action research does bridge this gap and unsettles our distinction.

Basically the relationship between research and action can take three forms: research prior to, during or subsequent to action (see Figure 2.1).

Research prior to action can be called "inventory research". Examples are: a study of the literature, a pilot study, or an experiment to investigate whether a certain action or a certain policy is sensible, has a chance of success, can actually be carried out, etc. Such research has a supportive character; it may be one of the determinants of the policy or line of action chosen. Of course, the research itself is certainly distinct from the action.

Research after the action is called "evaluation research". This research can take many forms, varying from administering a simple questionnaire or a few informal interviews to carrying out a well-prepared and empirically founded study. Of course, such an evaluation may in turn lead to some subsequent course of action (the design of a course, the approach in an organizational development programme) but, again, the research itself should be different from the object (the action) being evaluated.

Thirdly we can have research during the action, more enmeshed in action or policy. For this type of interaction the term "action research" is used. In the literature this term is anything but unequivocal. Interpretations vary from "a form of social group work" to "the only sensible form of social scientific research", or from "co-operation with those involved" to "societal revolution" (Wardekker, 1978).

Those seeking the common denominator of these opinions may end up with nothing but a few vaguely defined concepts.

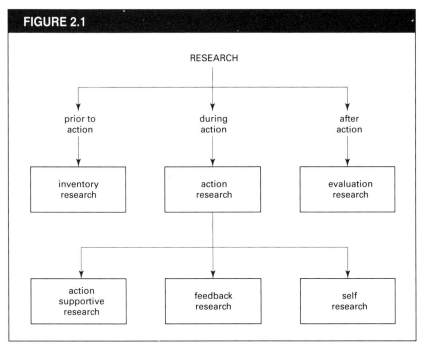

FIGURE 2.1

Relationship between research and actions.

In an attempt to further clarify the concept three forms of action research may be distinguished. In the first place, there is what could be called "action-*supportive* research". Such research is built into the various phases of an action programme, forming the basis for the next step to be taken or for correcting the course of a plan of action (Clark, 1972). It also includes a "norm orientation", which is deduced from the goal of the action. The research is always aimed at finding out to what extent the goal or sub-goal of the action has been or will be reached. But it is still research. This means that the conclusions of the research are not determined by the norms and values of the action or operation, but only by the empirical or logical evidence about whether or not the action goals have been achieved. Of course, it is desirable to have an independent third party carry out the study. Not without reason is a poll of the electorate carried out by the party bureau suspect.

It should be pointed out that the related term "regulative cycle" as proposed by Van Strien (1975), distinguishing the phases "research question — diagnosis — plan — intervention — evaluation" is not essentially different from the classical scientific cycle of: "problem definition — design — hypotheses — experiment — data-analysis — interpretation" (see, for instance, De Groot, 1971; Runkel & McGrath, 1972). The "plan" and "intervention" in the regulative cycle are derived from the action purpose and not from theoretical presuppositions, but this difference is completely in line with the distinction between applied and purely scientific research as we saw earlier.

In many cases it is probably correct to say that action-supportive research is focused primarily on individual, concrete cases, and consequently is a matter of application rather than applied research. "Generalizability" is, indeed, one of the biggest problems in action research. But this is not necessarily true. This type of research can indeed be used to generate general laws and to discover general knowledge, and this justifies its being called scientific research.

In the second form of action research, "feedback research", persons, groups or organizations are studied more closely by confronting them with the actual research and involving them in the

interpretation process. At the individual level this procedure can, for instance, be found in the use of test results as the starting point for a joint process of interpretation and further counselling treatment (see, for instance, Goldman, 1961). The so-called self-confrontation technique, an interview method developed by Hermans (1988), also abandons relationships being dominated by the psychologist/researcher, in that the subject of the research is most influential in determining what and how he/she prefers to communicate. At group level this principle was further elaborated by researchers at the University of Michigan in the "Survey Feedback Method" (Mann, 1957; Seashore & Bowers, 1964; Klein, Kraut & Wolfson, 1971), and by Heller in his "Group Feedback Analysis" (Heller, 1960, 1970, 1976).

In the GFA method, a certain measurement (of, for instance, job satisfaction or appreciation of the style of a leader) is carried out within certain groups (task forces, decision-making groups), often using questionnaires. The averaged scores are then fed back to the group and form the starting point for discussion. At the end of this discussion session the questionnaires are again filled out and analysed. Thus, the original scores, the second series of scores and the difference scores between these two points of measurement are available.

Heller lists three goals of GFA; first, validation of results; second, qualitative enrichment of the data; and third, stimulating change. It is the third goal in particular, acting as an agent of change, that makes this method a typical action research instrument in the strictest sense: research that motivates change, and in which those involved in this change process also participate. Discussions about scale scores and confrontations with others' scores are often a source of inspiration for making efforts towards changing and improving the situation.

A third form of action research is "self research" (Albinski, 1978). This type shows even more strongly the elements usually considered essential to action research: immediate usefulness to those involved, participation by the individuals and parties involved, and a focus on social change. In this third form of action research, the person or group involved participates not only in the interpretation of the data, but also in the setting up and carrying out of the study. This method originated in community work, where it is called "community self-survey" (MMW, 1960). Self-research is the beginning of a change process. The group itself sets up and carries out the study, promoting responsibility and democratization by means of awareness, self-diagnosis, and motivation. The role of the researcher has shifted to that of consultant, counsellor, and assistant. Obviously, the borderline between research and action is often overstepped, as the importance conferred upon self-activity and the involvement of individuals or groups comes to override that of the accuracy of data and conclusions. Of course, in such cases it is no longer possible to speak of research.

5 THE SCIENTIFIC INTERPRETATION PROCESS: SPECIAL PROBLEMS

A variety of problems are inherent in the process of scientific interpretation and drawing conclusions based on empirical data, especially for W&O psychology. The most significant of these will be discussed in this paragraph.

5.1 Analysing longitudinal data
In W&O psychology questions concerning both the nature and determinants of work behavioural phenomena are central. Why are some people more satisfied with their jobs than others? What are the causes of absenteeism in a company?

Understanding causal relationships allows for intelligently influencing the world. As was stated earlier, it is not sufficient to know that two phenomena have a statistical relationship. Before concluding a causal relationship, three other requirements must be met:

- the supposed cause-effect relationship must be theoretically plausible;
- the relationship must not disappear when a third variable is introduced into the analysis;
- the causal variable must precede the effect variable.

In *longitudinal* or *panel* research the same

people (the panel) are questioned several times, usually employing a (practically) identical questionnaire. Thus, the third requirement for causality (cause precedes effect) is met easily; naturally, one is certain that a variable measured at a certain point in time cannot be caused by a variable measured later. Therefore, longitudinal research is especially useful when one seeks to research causal relationships and/or to study the course of processes over time. This is not to say that these goals could never be met using data collected at a single moment in time (so-called *cross-sectional data*), but in that case it is even more imperative that there is only one possible interpretation for an observed relationship. After all, the direction of the causal relation must be absolutely unambiguous, and in cross-sectional research the design of studies usually does not allow for conclusions on this direction. In the following section, several types of longitudinal research which are often used in W&O psychology are discussed.

5.1.1. The discrete-time design
When data are collected at two points (at least) in time, with a period without measurement in between, we speak of *discrete-time* panel research. People could, for instance, be questioned about their job twice, with a one-year interval. Often, identical questions will be asked, in order to establish changes in opinions, values and attitudes. Next, one will want to determine the actual causes of these changes. Sometimes this question can be answered solely on the basis of theoretical insight and the sequence of variables in time. In other cases this can prove more difficult. A positive relationship could, for instance, exist between satisfaction with the organization and effectiveness of work consultation. The question, then, arises: Does effective consultation cause satisfaction or does effective consultation only become possible when one is satisfied with the company?

In these types of situation the use of *cross-lagged panel design* can be a solution (see Figure 2.2). At least two measurements at different points in time (T1 and T2) of the same two variables (A and B) are required.

According to this model, the score on A at time 2 is influenced by the score on A at time 1 (a

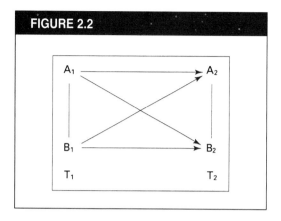

FIGURE 2.2

Cross-lagged panel analysis.

stability effect), as well as by the score on B at time 1. For variable B *mutatis mutandis* the same holds. If the crosswise effect of A1 on B2 is found to be larger than the effect of B1 on A2, then, under certain conditions, the conclusion is warranted that A causes B.

Interest in this model was mainly aroused by the work done by Campbell and Stanley (1963), who proposed to compare these crosswise correlation coefficients. Among others Kessler and Greenberg (1981) showed that this can easily lead to the wrong conclusions and therefore they recommend to compare standardized regression coefficients. Furthermore, they mention several other serious limitations of cross-lagged panel analysis. For a more extensive review of these limitations we refer to the relevant literature (see, for instance, Hagenaars, 1990).

Difference scores offer a second possibility.

A change in certain variables during the studied period seems easily measured by subtracting the score at time 2 from the score at time 1. The result shows the magnitude and direction of the observed change. This difference score can be related to other variables, for instance to check which people or groups underwent certain changes, or to find out to which other phenomena these changes are related.

Difference scores are attractive due to their simplicity, comprehensibility and—at face value— direct relevance. Nevertheless their application was heavily criticized on methodological grounds for a long period of time; many even refrained

from using this type of research method (see, for instance, Cronbach & Furby, 1970). The most important criticisms concerned:

1. The *unreliability* of difference scores. The difference between two variables is usually less reliable than the two separate variables.
2. The occurrence of *ceiling* effects. People with a high score at time 1 will improve less in the second measurement than people with a lower first score. The higher the score at time 1 the less room for improvement at time 2.
3. The occurrence of *regression* effects. People with either extremely high or extremely low scores on the first measurement will often, at time 2, score somewhat lower or higher respectively, due to chance factors. Therefore, a high score at time 1 will often have a negative correlation with the difference score. And, other variables correlating positively with the score at time 1, will then also correlate negatively with the difference scores. This negative correlation has no substantive meaning and is merely caused by methodological artefacts.

However, over the last decade the attitude towards the use of difference scores has changed. Several important authors (for instance, Allison, 1990; Burke & Nesselroade, 1990) place the criticisms in perspective and stipulate under which conditions the use of difference scores leads to acceptable results. They observe that using difference scores can often be very meaningful. However, all this depends on the specification of the model. To further extend on this topic is beyond the scope of this chapter; the reader is referred to, for instance, Allison (1990).

An important problem within the discrete time approach is that the magnitude of effects depends on the length of the period in between the measurements. Carsten and Spector (1987), for example, in their meta analysis of the relationship between satisfaction and organizational commitment on the one hand and turnover on the other, found that the strength of this relationship decreased as the time period between measurements increased. In general, the influence of the length of the period between measurements on the strength of effects is highly unpredictable. Effects can weaken, or sometimes become stronger: even the direction of the effect can change (Sandefur & Tuma, 1987). Strictly speaking this means that results obtained for a given period are not generalizable to periods of a different length; conclusions found for a period of, for example, one year can not be considered valid for a period of two years. We hereby touch on a major limitation of the discrete-time design. The relevant literature therefore proposes to use, if possible, a continuous-time design rather than a discrete-time design.

5.1.2   The continuous-time design: event history analysis

In this type of research data are collected concerning the development of a variable during a certain period, instead of measuring the scores on this variable at two or more points in time. An easy way to obtain this kind of data is to question people about the past (so-called retrospective questions). Of course, this is not equally sensible for all types of variables; asking people to indicate, for instance, how satisfied they were with their job two years ago will prove rather useless. After all, people will often have forgotten, and the chance of mistakes or distortions is large. Highly unreliable results will therefore be obtained for this type of question.

Other kinds of variables could lead to different results. For instance, most people have a correct recollection of the course of their educational and professional careers, including the various dates, especially when one does not go back in time too far. More in general, one can state that data on *qualitative* change (changing from having a job to being unemployed, from one job to the other etc.) can usually be obtained rather well through retrospective questions. This method is less useful for *quantitative* changes (for instance, from more to less happy, satisfied etc.). Thus, the continuous- and discrete-time design are often combined: some variables are measured using the continuous-time design (qualitative changes, such as the development course of professional careers); for other variables the discrete-time design is used. Such a procedure combines the strengths of both approaches.

To analyse continuous-time data concerning qualitative change, several statistical procedures have been proposed, the so-called *survival*, *course*, or *event history* techniques. These techniques relate the probability of someone undergoing a certain qualitative change (such as from employed to unemployed, from going to school to having a job) to explaining variables. In contrast with the discrete-time design, the exact moment at which the transition from the one state to the other occurred, is known in continuous-time design. This means that parameter estimates are no longer dependent on the length of the period between measurements. Even observations, where no transition has (yet) occurred at the cessation of the period of data collection, can be used to estimate parameters. This makes event history analysis a statistically well advanced method for the analyses of continuous-time data.

There are, however several practical problems with this method. Often one needs to provide a certain distribution of the chance of a transition in advance. One could, for instance, suppose that the chance of changing jobs decreases, remains constant or maybe even increases the longer respondents have the same job (see Blossfeld, Hamerle & Mayer, 1989). In the social sciences there is often little reason to *a priori* presuppose such distributions. In such instances the semi-parametrical approach as proposed by Cox (1972) can be helpful. This approach does not require *a priori* specification of the chance that a transition will occur, but deduces this chance from the data.

Another important problem with event history analysis is that the scores for the explaining variables are supposed to be known for the entire duration of the observation period. This is, of course, always true for stable variables such as sex, socio-economic status and date of birth, neither will this present problems for variables such as prestige of a profession, age or tenure. However, it is hard to meet this requirement for norms, values and attitudes (e.g. satisfaction and commitment to the organization). This means that the estimation of the effects of this type of inconstant variables can be seriously distorted. In practice, it is often recommendable, when researching the effects of variables such as commitment to the organization and job satisfaction on turnover, to hark back to the discrete-time panel design that was discussed before (Taris, 1994, reviews this topic more extensively).

5.2   Levels of analysis

Multi-level analysis is a technique with which observed behaviour of individuals is explained from the characteristics of these individuals, as well as from characteristics of the group or groups to which they belong. For an explanation of the production rate of employees one can think of individual variables, such as motivation or demographic characteristics (age, sex), but also of workgroup level variables such as the educational level that was required in the recruitment of personnel. At departmental level one can think of the remuneration system which could influence motivation. And at the organizational level the influence of organizational culture or the general personnel policies can be mentioned as an example.

Although multi-level research is still mostly practised in educational research at this point in time, W&O psychology seems another fruitful area for the application of multi-level research, given the hierarchical structure of many organizations and the presuppositions of multi-level research.

The central idea of multi-level research is that the behaviour of individuals is not only regulated by individual characteristics, but also by characteristics of the environment. The assumption is that there is a hierarchical organizational structure, although the boundaries between the different levels do not necessarily have to be clear-cut. Recruitment policies regarding educational requirements for personnel, for instance, could be identical for several work units and employees could belong to more than one unit.

In the context of educational research Van den Eeden and Meijnen (1990) point out that the prevailing opinion is that variables at the higher level are the independent and variables at the lower level, the dependent variables. This, however, does not necessarily have to be correct. The direction of a causal relationship is not necessarily top-down; the reverse is also possible. For instance, low motivation among workers (lower level) can lead to a management decision (higher level) to change the required level of education.

Thinking in terms of our example, the application of multi-level research could lead to the separation of personal and organizational variables influencing production. On these grounds, conclusions can then be drawn about, for example, the effectiveness of measures at the organizational level in relation to production figures. A possible conclusion could be that level of education is important to productivity, but that culture is not. Moreover, in this type of analysis, an averaged productivity figure as the only indication of the quality of work units is not meaningful, as it is not known then to which extent work performance is caused by personal or by environmental variables. The use of multi-level analysis can clarify this type of issue.

The general scheme underlying multi-level research can be described as follows. First one attempts to describe the relations between variables at the same level. For instance, using a regression model the productivity score of individual employees is predicted from their motivation scores or other possible individual variables. As in regular regression analyses, a better prediction can be obtained through adding extra predictors in the model. The reverse route can also be taken, whereby a complex model is simplified step by step through leaving out weak predictors. Such analyses must be carried out for different work units, because it would otherwise not be possible to use characteristics of work units to explain productivity.

For each work unit estimates of the intercept parameter and the slope parameters (regression coefficients) are obtained. The intercept parameter provides an indication of the general productivity level for each work unit. The slope parameter gives an indication of the strength of the relation between motivation and productivity. After studying the relation between motivation and productivity at the individual level, one attempts to explain variance in both the intercepts and slopes across units in terms of a situational higher level variable (in the present example the average level of education of recruited employees). Two regression equations can be drawn using average level of education as predictor: one in which the intercept, and one in which the slope is predicted. In this analysis it comes down to—characteristic for multi-level analyses—first transforming the relations among variables at the "person" level (motivation, production) to group characteristics (intercept, slope), which, then, are explained in terms of variables that are measured at the group level in question (required level of education).

As this chapter is meant to have an introductory character, we will not further interpret the parameters estimated at the second level of analysis. The reader is referred to, for instance, Bosker and Snijders (1990) and Fife-Schaw (ch. 4 in Breakwell et al., 1995). We would, however, like to remark that usually the estimation of regression model parameters at different levels does not take place separately, but on basis of a single regression model—the multi-level model—which includes the separate variables as well as the interaction terms. The structure of the residual component is more complicated in this model than in a normal regression model, in which the explicit distinction between levels is not made.

As mentioned, due to the explicit hierarchical structure in educational systems—students, classes, schools, types of schools—multi-level research is most popular in present-day educational research. But, again, other types of organizations—both commercial and non- profit—also seem suitable grounds for the application of the multi-level approach, as long as an hierarchical structure in the organization, and thus in the independent variables, can be assumed. In many cases, defending such an assumption seems warranted.

5.3 The "third factor"

In the complex field of W&O psychological research, where the relation between two variables X and Y is studied, there is often a third variable, Z, that influences two variables, X and Y, and possibly their interrelationship. Figure 2.3 presents four common cases. In the following discussion the nature of the influence of this variable Z and the way in which it can be identified will be analysed.

a. Intervening variable. First, the relationship between X and Y can be caused or strengthened by a third variable Z, when this variable has the character of an intervening variable. X influences

Z and Z influences Y, and thus (part of) the interrelationship between X and Y is caused by the functioning of Z (see Figure 2.3a). An example: height (X) and playing basketball (Z) are related. In basketball there are relatively many ankle injuries (Y). One could therefore find a correlation between height and ankle injuries. However, it would be incorrect to conclude that these two variables have an intrinsic relationship. The influence of intervening variable Z or, inversely, the true relationship between X and Y, can be identified by calculating the partial correlation between X and Y keeping Z constant.

b. Element in a circular chain. This model is illustrated in Figure 2.3b. X influences Z, Z influences Y, and in its turn Y influences X. (Naturally, the influence of the causal chain can

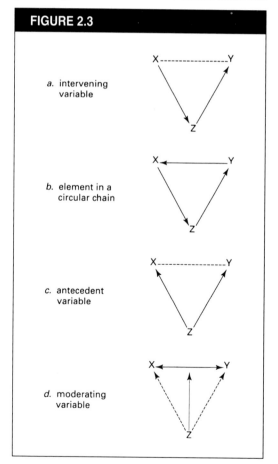

FIGURE 2.3

a. intervening variable

b. element in a circular chain

c. antecedent variable

d. moderating variable

Different ways in which Z possibly influences the relation between X–Y.

also run in the reverse direction.) To give an example: increasing the influence of a consultative body (X) can result in attracting better people (Y) to this body, which could improve the quality of decisions taken (Z). This could again lead to an increase in the influence given to the consultative body, etc. It is often hard to discern the "starting point" of this circle, and the correlations usually only provide a complex pattern. Interpretation needs to be led by theoretical insight.

c. *Antecedent variable*. This model (Figure 2.3c) is frequently found in the social sciences and is often responsible for incorrect interpretations of detected relationships. Antecedent variables are also called "confounding" variables. An example from research in developing countries: socio-economic status (Z) has a negative relation with the number of children per family (X), and a positive relation with the number of books per family (Y). Consequently, the more books the less children. It would obviously be nonsense to think that a real and interpretable relationship between these two variables X and Y exists, let alone that the one would determine the other (the more books one reads, the less children one has). In this case, again, partial correlations keeping Z constant reveal the true relationships.

d. *Moderating variables*. The ground principle of a moderating variable (see Figure 2.3d) is that it, although not necessarily being correlated with two other variables, influences the relationship between these two variables. There need not be a correlation between the nature of the task (Z) and participative leadership (X) on the one hand or with the satisfaction with this style of leadership (Y) on the other. However, the nature of the task could still influence the relationship between the leadership style and its appreciation (for instance, this relation is stronger for task-related than for personnel-related decisions (Drenth & Koopman, 1984). In a regression equation for the prediction of Y this will be revealed through a significant contribution of the interaction term XZ, which is, therefore the method suggested in the literature to identify moderating variables (Saunders, 1956). A simpler method, often used for categorical variables, is "subgrouping" in which the total popu-

lation is subdivided on the basis of possible moderators (male–female, indigenous–foreign ethnic groups) and it is examined whether divergent correlations between X and Y exist within the different subgroups.

It is not necessary for a moderator Z to be unrelated to X or Y. Z can also contribute to the prediction of Y on its own, apart from being a moderator. In that case the linear additive model is combined with the multiplicative model, using the formula: $Y = aX + bZ + cXZ$, in which a and b are the Beta-weights for X and Z respectively, and c is the Beta-weight for the interaction term XZ.

5.4 Types of error

In the following an overview is given of interpretation and conclusion *errors* that can disrupt the scientific interpretation process. Four categories are discussed.

1.   Error, based on incorrect or insufficient *operationalizations* of used concepts. There are two possible types: first, measures can be insufficiently objective and reliable, and secondly, the chosen measurement instruments do not adequately reflect the constructs to be measured. The latter concerns the problem of construct validity of the instruments. It is possible that the instrument does not co-vary sufficiently with the behaviour or phenomenon it is supposed to measure (insufficient confirmative construct validity), that the instrument co-varies with other behaviour or another phenomenon with which it is not supposed to correlate (insufficient discriminatory validity; see Campbell & Fiske, 1959). For a discussion of the way to estimate these qualities and the technical solutions to further the reliability and validity, one is referred to the literature on this topic (Nunnally, 1967; Campbell, 1976; Drenth & Sijtsma, 1990).

2.   Errors caused by incorrect *statistical* handling of data. The most important errors here can be categorized into two well-known types:

(a)   The null hypothesis is falsely rejected, that is, a relationship or causality is wrongly assumed to be proven.

(b) The null hypothesis is falsely accepted, in other words, the relationship or causality is wrongly judged to be *absent*.

Several statistical missteps can be considered to cause the first aforementioned type of error, including a low level of significance, testing one-tailed rather than two-tailed or the use of insensitive tests. On the contrary the second type of error could be caused by a high level of significance, testing double-sided instead of single-sided or using oversensitive tests.

An error of the first type is often made in W&O psychology in exploratory research in which a great number of relations is studied. This results in an increased chance that significant relations are found "accidentally". When one hundred relations are studied, according to the distribution of chance we will always find five of these to be significant at the 5% level.

Often the error of the second type is caused by undersized samples. Especially in organizational psychology one often has to depend on too small samples as at the chosen level of aggregation (organizations) large enough samples are hardly ever feasible. For the discussion of statistical errors we again refer to the existing methodological handbooks (Hays, 1963; Edwards, 1965; Kerlinger, 1973; Cook & Campbell, 1979; Breakwell et al., 1995).

3. Error based on insufficient *internal validity*. The most important question regarding internal validity is whether the results can indeed be attributed to the factors one deems responsible based on the research results (in an experiment these are the independent variables). When, for instance, a different reward system is introduced in a department and from comparative research (measurement before and after) it is concluded that people enjoy going to work more and that absenteeism drops, the internal validity question is whether these results can indeed be attributed to the independent variable, i.e. the reward system. Cook and Campbell (1976, 1979; see also the updated version by Cook, Campbell & Peracchio, 1990) present a systematic overview of the threats to internal validity which we will follow in the discussion hereafter.

- History: did something else happen which is responsible for the results (for example, a raise in salary)?
- Maturation: was the result caused by normal adaptation and growth processes which would also have occurred without intervening in the reward system?
- Testing: did the measurement itself cause the change (employees get attention, enjoy the research activities, the well-known Hawthorne-effect)?
- Instrumentation: did the effect result from the fact that the second measurement was not identical to the first or was influenced by the first measurement? Often recollection and recognition effects play a part in the second measurement.
- Statistical regression: if measurements are not very reliable, high scorers will usually score lower and low scorers will score higher in the second measurement, due to the statistical regression phenomenon.
- Selection: the group participating in the study is positively or negatively biased.
- Mortality: a non-random part of the research group drop-out during the course of the experiment.
- Interaction with selection; many of these threats to internal validity can interact with selection to produce forces that might spuriously be seen as effects of the experimental change.

In a classically and well-designed experiment (see later on) a control group is always chosen whose results are compared with those of the experimental group. This naturally provides a substantially better insight than measuring the change within a single group. However, in this design several other threats are posed to internal validity.

- Diffusion, that is the control group also grows familiar with the experimental condition, raising the question whether the control group is indeed non-experimental.
- Rivalry between the experimental and control group, with resultant positive or negative effects.

- Demoralization of the control group that does not receive the experimental condition. After all, this condition is supposed to be positive, since otherwise it would not be studied. This is a serious problem in, for instance, medical pharmaceutical research, in which a control group is not prescribed "beneficial" medication. This example also shows that in this type of research there is, besides the problem of demoralization of the control group, an additional ethical problem involved: the question whether it is justified to withhold something desirable from a group of subjects.
- Local history: accidental events that do take place in one but not in the other group and could influence the comparison.

4.   Errors due to inadmissible *generalization* of results (described as "external validity" by Cook & Campbell). With this kind of error one incorrectly generalizes to situations outside the given research context. In a specific research context three facets can be distinguished across which one must generalize: (1) the research conditions (in the example mentioned under sub-head 3, for example, the type of reward system, which department, what kind of work), (2) the method of observation (satisfaction assessment through questionnaires? which absenteeism-index?), and (3) the studied people or objects (is the research sample of employees representative for the total work population of the firm?).

It will be clear in light of the above that especially conclusions from case studies allow little generalization. However experimental laboratory studies can also be problematic in this respect. The external validity question here focuses on the "reality value" of the obtained results in real life situations. Bronfenbrenner (1977) has called this source of error lack of "ecological validity".

5.5   Meta analysis

A relatively new method, that became influential almost immediately after its origination, is the so-called meta analysis. Meta analysis is a quantitative method used to integrate a large amount of studies on the same topic. With the increasing

number of reported findings from scientific research and the often encountered contradictory findings on a single subject, this method aims to provide a systematic synthesis of these various publications. The assumption underlying the method of meta analysis is that such a systematic integration of existing studies is more valuable than conducting yet another study, which is hoped to finally provide a definitive answer to a certain research question that, one feels, has not been answered sufficiently by the research done so far.

The term meta analysis was introduced by Glass (1976), who first used this method in research concerning the effects of psychotherapy. This publication gave rise to the further development and refinement of the method by several researchers. This development has sometimes been accompanied by vehement debates between advocates and opponents of certain solutions. We can now conclude that there is consensus about several essential issues and that meta analysis has found its place among the acknowledged repertory of research methods. The influence of this method nowadays extends into all social sciences and is also visible outside the social sciences, for instance, in biological and medical research (see Goodman, 1991).

The goal of a meta analysis is usually twofold (Rosenthal, 1991). First, one wishes to combine the results of all gathered studies into a single value. This value then represents an estimate of the population value. An example is obtaining an estimate of the relation between job satisfaction and job performance by combining all separate results from the gathered studies into a weighted mean correlation. Secondly, one wants to study the variation in the results of different studies. Relations between job satisfaction and job performance could, for instance, be influenced by a hypothesized third variable (a task or organizational characteristic, see section 5.3). This third variable could cause the variation in results in the different studies. The observed variation could also have statistical origins. One can think of, for instance, sampling errors, such as the effect of using small samples.

In W&O psychology the method of meta analysis was put into action from a specific perspective. This initiative was taken relatively independent of the aforementioned development which started with the publication by Glass. Still, both resultant approaches correspond with each other to a large extent (see Hunter & Schmidt, 1991). The method used within W&O psychology was developed by Hunter and Schmidt, who, in the same period that Glass developed his method, were intensively engaged in answering the question to which extent, in various studies in the area of selection, relationships found between test scores of applicants and their job performance were compatible for similar tests and occupations. Thus, they compared reported validity coefficients. Their assumption was that the differences between the reported validity coefficients for a certain type of test—for instance, general intelligence tests—and for a given type of occupation or job—for instance, clerical jobs—mainly originated from methodological artefacts, and did not refer to intrinsic situational differences between jobs (differences in organizations, work groups, regions, etc.). In order to reflect this, they corrected the observed variance in validity coefficients for a number of artefacts such as sampling error, differences in reliability of both predictors and criteria, and differences in restriction of range. If only little variance in the validity coefficients would remain after controlling for these artefacts, one can speak of a group of homogeneous coefficients and conclude to validity generalization, according to this line of thought. In other words, the validity is, in that case, generalizable over specific situations (organizations, regions, etc.). This enabled them to speak of, for instance, "the" validity of general intelligence tests for clerical functions. Naturally, the underlying motive for Hunter and Schmidt was the desire to be able to use psychological tests without having to calculate the predictive validity for every separate selection goal and in every specific selection situation. Through their approach they challenged the prevailing supposition that predictive validity is always situationally specific.

Their meta analysis method has to date not only been used to study validity generalization, but has also been used for questions outside selection psychology, for instance, for questions pertaining to absenteeism, turnover, job satisfaction, role conflict, role ambiguity, leadership styles, and personnel appraisal (see Hunter & Schmidt, 1991). From many of these meta analyses it was concluded that an important part of the observed variance in research results can be attributed to methodological artefacts (especially sampling error), but that in some cases part of the variance can also be explained intrinsic by differences on theoretically meaningful variables.

Characteristic for the method developed by Hunter and Schmidt is the emphasis on correcting the observed variance in results for different sorts of methodological artefacts. One of the most important differences between this method and the one developed by Glass as well as other meta analytical methods is the explicit stress on obtaining a compilation of homogeneous research results through using methods for correction. Other meta analysts often pay more attention to studying theoretically relevant moderators.

An important issue in meta analysis (see, for instance, Durlak & Lipsey, 1991) is that the topic should be well-defined, in order to leave no obscurity about the criteria for the selection of studies that will or will not be used in the analyses. Gathering these studies should be done in a systematic manner, in which it is important to also include non-published material (the so-called "grey" literature, such as papers presented at congresses). Coding of research characteristics can be difficult: sometimes a certain result can be placed in more than one category. The criteria used to make such decisions should therefore be made explicit. A final important part of a meta analytical study is the conversion of different primary research data into values of one and the same measure. Often, a measure for the magnitude of the effect, such as Cohen's so-called "d"-measure or the correlation coefficient is used for that purpose.

When conducting statistical analyses, it is important, among other things, to systematically estimate the heterogeneity of the compiled effect sizes. Both methodological arguments and theoretical expectations derived beforehand can play a role in this process. The more heterogeneous, the less meaningful the overall average of results from the different studies will be.

When interpreting results from meta analyses it is important to realize that a meta analysis always contains a number of subjective decisions (see also Wanouw, Sullivan & Malinak, 1989). After superficially studying the meta analytical method one sometimes wrongly assumes that the quantitative character of the method has completely eliminated subjectivity. The fact that meta analyses on the same topic can yield contradictory results (see, for instance, Petty, McGee & Cavender, 1984; Iaffaldano & Muchinsky, 1985) shows that this has not been achieved. Moreover, there are disputes about the way one needs to treat studies of poor quality in meta analysis and about the extent to which studies combined in one meta analysis are indeed compatible (the problem of comparing apples and oranges). Also, meta analysts still disagree with each other about the correct way to establish the degree to which the used results of research studies are heterogeneous. Finally, some meta analysts have been criticized for using several, non-independent results from one and the same study, which causes that study to have a higher weight in the meta analysis than other studies (for instance, using results from the same sample in three different age categories from a single study). Despite these points of discussion and controversies the conclusion that the method of meta analysis is a highly influential development within a wide range of studies seems warranted.

For a further study of this method we refer to Hedges and Olkin (1985), Wolff (1986), Hunter and Schmidt (1990, 1991), Durlak and Lipsey (1991) and Rosenthal and Rosnov (1991). Computer programs for meta analysis have, among others, been developed by Schwarzer (1989) and Hunter and Schmidt (1990).

6   DIFFERENCES IN RESEARCH DESIGN

In this paragraph the different possibilities to design a study in the field of W&O psychology are discussed. We will limit ourselves to empirical studies (see Figure 2.4).

A first distinction refers to the difference between studying behaviour that is evoked by an experimental condition, in which the setting of the study is therefore of primary importance, and

behaviour that is evoked by stimuli (questions, tasks, tests), in which this is not the case.

To start with the latter type of research design: there are two forms of research where the experimental setting is not crucial. In the first place, so-called *survey research*, in which the researcher is interested in the strength of preferences (for instance, in consumer research or political polls) or attitudes (towards a leader's work aspects, a new pension plan, etc.). Often the level of processing of this type of data is of a simple uni- or bivariate character (distributions of frequencies, differences between groups); however, this is not necessarily the case. More complicated multivariate data processing designs are possible as well, such as higher order analyses of variance, taxonomic analyses and others. In survey research the selection of respondents is the central issue.

One can also be interested in the nature of a *phenomenon*. Whether job satisfaction is a uni- or multidimensional concept, which layout of displays or control panels leads to the least errors in perception or reaction, how technical insight is related to on the one hand intelligence and on the other training and experience, whether safety behaviour is more dependent on the "safety" qualities of machines and tools than on personality factors or characteristics of the environment... these kinds of question require an analysis of a carefully selected sample of stimuli. Obviously these stimuli must then be "administered" to a sample of respondents (which presents a restriction to generalizability), in order that conclusions can be drawn from (the pattern of) reactions about the psychological phenomenon under study.

Next, there is empirical research in which the experimental condition or "setting", is indeed of decisive importance. Regarding this experimental condition a further distinction can be made between on the one hand a condition created especially for the purpose of the study and on the other existing, given circumstances that are treated as experimental conditions. The latter refers to the what is called a *field study*.

An example of these two forms: the question whether an intensive four-month typing course yields results inferior to those of a less intensive six-month course could be studied by comparing the results of two experimentally designed

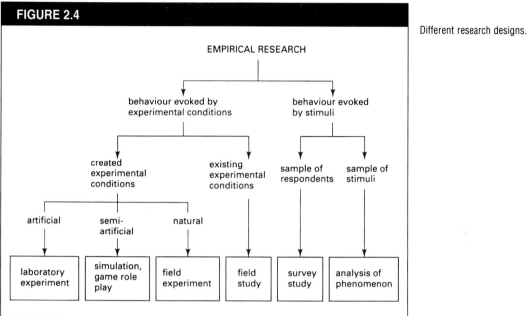

Different research designs.

courses, one lasting six and the other four months. However, this study could also be performed using results obtained from two existing four- or six-month courses to obtain the diploma in question that are taught as usual.

Within the design in which an experimental setting is created, there are three possibilities: an artificial condition, a semi-artificial condition and a natural condition. In the first case we are dealing with a *laboratory experiment*. The experimental condition is completely artificial, as the experiment takes place in a laboratory in order to control for the abundance of influencing variables present in a natural setting. In the third case we are dealing with a *field experiment*. Although the experimental condition is indeed especially created for the study, the natural character of the situation that is to be observed is left in tact as much as possible. In an organization, a new reward system (for instance, a group related system), is introduced in one department whereas in another department, which is selected on the basis of its similarity to the former, the reward system (individual performance related pay) is not changed. The differences in the reaction to both reward systems are registered and form the basis for the evaluation of the new system.

Between these two experimental designs there is a third form, the so-called semi-artificial research designs, including simulations, games and role playing. None of these is entirely artificial, as in varying degrees, the natural setting is imitated. On the other hand none of these is completely natural either, as this imitation remains an incomplete reflection of real-life situations.

Within the semi-artificial design there are three distinguishable types which vary in their level of manipulation of the conditions. First, one could, in principle, continuously manipulate the external conditions during the experiment. We are then dealing with *simulation*, a procedure, for that matter, which is used more often in training and for educational purposes than in experimental research (Gagné, 1962). When only the situation at the start of the experiment is determined and the participants themselves are delegated the control over the parameters thereafter, we speak of "games"; in an organizational setting these are called business games. An example of research regarding decision making through budgeting games is found in the study of Hofstede (1967). Through computer aided processing there are countless mixed or intermediate forms of these types of simulations available nowadays. Not only the situation at the start but also many other adaptations and external influences, some controlled by participants and others outside their control, can be introduced into the game, thereby increasing the game's realism.

A third type of semi-artificial research involves *role play*. Participants are asked to pretend they are fulfilling a certain role. This precondition of "pretending" is obviously at the same time the weak point of these types of experiment (Freedman, 1969). For an overview of the possibilities and limitations of semi-artificial experimental research, see Fromkin and Streufert (1976).

Many discussions have taken place concerning the meaning and usefulness of the laboratory experiment as compared with the field experiment and field study. In this discussion the semi-artificial experiments usually have an intermediate position. Interesting to W&O psychology is Locke's (1986) observation that field and laboratory experiments can yield highly similar conclusions.

In defence of the value of laboratory experiments, two major problems inherent in field experiments and field studies should be noticed. First, it is impossible to control for (often many) unwanted influences. Second, it is impossible, often due to practical reasons, to meet the requirement of comparability of groups, departments, or organizations in the experimental condition on the one hand, and the control condition on the other. And, the latter is an important requirement. After all, if one wants to draw conclusions about the effect of the experimental variable (for instance, task enrichment) from a comparison of the reactions in an experimental department (task enrichment introduced) and a control department (existing short cycle tasks), then one must be certain that potential differences are not caused by other factors than the intended condition. In other words, the threats to internal validity are large; on the one hand because it is impossible to eliminate unwanted influences, and on the other hand because it is impossible to find perfectly comparable research groups or to randomly distribute persons over the two conditions.

The major drawback of the laboratory experiment, however, is its artificial nature. The circumstances often have little in common with the real life situation, thus decreasing the reality value of the results (i.e. the external, or ecological validity). This is particularly problematic with more complex processes that need to be understood in their special social and organisational context. It is for this reason that cross-cultural studies deserve special attention in this respect (see, for instance, Lonner & Berry, 1986). In other words, in laboratory experiments confidence in the accuracy of the insight in causal relations increases, at the expense of the generalizability and realism of this knowledge. For each separate case one will have to determine whether confidence regarding the accuracy of the conclusions and the reality value of the results are in a proper balance.

As stated, in field experiments there is seldom, and in field studies hardly ever the possibility to randomly distribute research subjects over the different experimental and control conditions. Thus, one cannot speak of a "real" experiment, in which this randomization is essential (besides controlling unwanted influences). However, Cook and Campbell (1976, 1979), and Cook, Campbell and Peracchio (1990) present several conditions under which field experiments and field studies can nevertheless be referred to as "experiments", including the possibility to infer causal relationships. Studies meeting these requirements are not called "real", but quasi-experiments.

We will now present several of the most common quasi-experimental possibilities as described by Cook and Campbell. First and foremost is that without the availability of a control group, it is simply impossible to speak of an experimental study. This immediately excludes two types of research designs that are nevertheless often used in the practice of W&O psychology, namely:

one-group posttest-only design
one-group pretest-posttest design

When the experimental condition is denominated with X and the observation with O, then the following models are not acceptable:

$X\, O$ and $O_1\, X\, O_2$

The first model is certainly not acceptable since as

one has no idea whether any kind of change took place at all, and if it did, whether this resulted from the influence of X. However, the more frequently used second model (pretest observation—treatment—posttest observation) is also insufficient, as it is not known whether the observed changes were indeed caused by the condition X, rather than being the result of normal maturing or change processes that would have also taken place had the treatment X not been given. A good example is given by Wolff-Albers (1968), who showed that several observed changes in behaviour and performance of students of a Dutch business school could not be explained by changes introduced in its educational system and curriculum, because changes found in several other, comparable tertiary educational institutes in The Netherlands were just as large.

The most important and interpretable models described by Cook and Campbell are:

1. *The intreated control group design with pretest and posttest*

$$\frac{O_1 \ X \ O_2}{O_1 \ O_2}$$

The only difference with a laboratory experiment is that the "experimental" and control group are not matched or composed in an a-select way. Naturally, the quality of experiment in question increases, the more this ideal is met. In other words, in such an experiment it is important to choose departments, research groups, etc. as comparable as possible to ensure a maximal internal validity.

2. *The reversed-treatment nonequivalent control group design with pretest and posttest*

$$\frac{O_1 \ X+ \ O_2}{O_1 \ X- \ O_2}$$

The difference with the aforementioned design is that in this design in addition to the experimental group receiving the $X+$ treatment the control group also receives an experimental treatment. This treatment represents the conceptually opposite treatment $X-$, that is expected to lead to

reversed findings in the $X-$ group. For instance, higher versus lower pay, more participative versus more autocratic leadership, a higher versus a lower temperature.

3. *A one-group removed-treatment design with pretest and posttest*

$$O_1 \ X \ O_2 \quad O_3 \ \bar{X} \ O_4$$

A difference between O_1 and O_2 can be attributed to X (for instance, the introduction of music at work) with reasonable confidence, when the removal of the condition has a reverse effect in due time. O_3 does not necessarily have to be equal to O_2. Some natural developments (wear and tear, habitation) can of course take place, but after X a clear discontinuity in the observed scores should be noticed.

4. *A one-group repeated-treatment design with pretest and posttest*

$$O_1 \ X \ O_2 \ \bar{X} \ O_3 \ X \ O_4$$

An example of this design is the repeated administration of a certain stimulant (a stimulating condition or medicine). The outcomes of this design are most interpretable when both O_1 and O_2, and O_3 and O_4 differ from each other, and these differences are in the same direction.

These models are not airtight and do have certain shortcomings regarding internal validity (for a detailed review, see Cook and Campbell, 1979, chapter 3). Under certain circumstances and with certain outcomes, however, results are interpretable. One can indeed give explanations, even causal ones, based on these "not real experiments".

7 METHODS OF DATA COLLECTION

This chapter will be concluded with an overview of the different methods of data collection used in W&O psychology.

Generally speaking these methods can be classified from two points of view (see Figure 2.5).

Methods of data collection.

FIGURE 2.5

Channel / Structure	Structured	Unstructured
Subject	• questionnaires • scales • structured interviews • objectives tests	• open interviews • projection tests
Researcher	• systematic observation • ratings	• impressions • participative observation
Experts/others	• ratings/appraisals • interview schedules	• brainstorming • Delphi method
Registration/equipment	• indirect indication • experimental equipment	• video, film, tape
Archives	• recorded data	• personal documents • official documents

First, the *channel* through which information is received. This can be the subject being investigated; he or she is the one providing the data. Secondly, it can be the researcher him- or herself who produces data, for instance, by means of ratings or recording of impressions. Next, the information could originate from the judgement or opinion of a third party (an expert or a person involved). Furthermore, there is also the possibility of gathering information through objective registration or experimental equipment. Finally, information could, in principle, be available as it is stored in already existing documentation files and archives.

A second point of view from which methods can be classified is that of the extent to which the used *material* is structured. Some methods require a clear specification of which information is to be selected and how this information should be categorized before the actual collection of the data. These are called the structured methods. When selection and categorization of information takes place after data collection or does not take place at all, we speak of unstructured methods.

Using these two points of view, the various methods of data collection can be placed into a matrix as depicted in Figure 2.5.

A short description of all aforementioned methods will now be given.

7.1 Subject

In the first place, methods where the subject is the source of information. The following techniques within this category can be considered structured methods:

7.1.1 Questionnaires

These are filled out by the respondent (individually or collectively, in a personal meeting or by telephone, under supervision of a researcher or independently, for instance, when questionnaires are mailed to respondents). This frequently used tool has been discussed extensively in literature. For a review of the various questionnaire forms and the technical problems involved in the construction of questionnaires, see for instance, Oppenheim (1966), Bouchard (1976), Babbie (1979) and Meerling (1980).

7.1.2 Scales

Existing, but more often, specifically developed scales are used to measure certain attitude objects or social phenomena, such as satisfaction with all kinds of aspects of work (British Telecom, 1984a; Hulin, 1990), organizational characteristics (Van de Ven & Ferry, 1980, British Telecom, 1984b) or leadership (Bass, 1990).

7.1.3 Structured interviews

Structuring could apply to both the question and answering categories. This method strongly resembles the questionnaire method, although here the questions are filled out by the researcher. There is, of course, a certain latitude before a structured interview becomes an "open interview". For instance, the order of questions or the exact wording can be adapted to the subject or the research situation (Richardson et al., 1965). The research on and experiences with the interview as a method to obtain information (Kahn & Cannell, 1967; Flippo, 1971) or as a basis for decision making (Randell, 1978) and selection of personnel (Guion, 1990) have been thoroughly documented in literature.

7.1.4 Objective tests

A wide variety of tests measuring capacity or personality factors are available or can be constructed. With respect to this category of tests, we are referring to tests in which the evaluation of test performance or behaviour can be made in a relatively objective manner. This is definitely the case when using a multiple choice format, but not imposible through the use of open ended questions. For a critical survey of available tests, see Cronbach (1970), Buros (1978), or Aiken (1996).

The category of *unstructured* methods with the research subject as the channel of information consists of the following techniques:

7.1.5 Open interviews

The transition from the structured to the open interview is gradual and it is not easy to exactly define the border between the two. At the extremes it is quite clear. The open interview leaves the selection of topics in the interview and the order in which the topics are introduced, as well as the way the answers are recorded or categorized to the researcher. Whyte (1960) provided a detailed description of the advantages of this type of interview. The researcher often uses a tape recorder, analysing the tape after the interview. One of the major objections to the unstructured interview is the selectiveness of the choice of topics (Mayfield, 1964; Drenth, 1988), which results in a lack of systematic comparability.

7.1.6 Projection tests

Projection tests, in which subjects have to make up a story of their own on the basis of a depicted situation, or in which a reaction to a question or remark must be given in a "balloon" (as in cartoons), also provide unstructured material which has to be interpreted by the researcher. In psychodiagnostics these methods have been in use for a long time (Anderson & Anderson, 1951), although they have been heavily criticized. This method has also been used in attitude research (Campbell,1950) and motivation studies (Atkinson, 1958; Drenth, 1960). Most frequently, however, these methods were applied in research into consumer preferences and attitudes (Smith, 1954; Katona, 1960). Just as in diagnostics, these techniques are primarily appropriate in the first phase of a study, in which the emphasis lays on the generation of ideas and hypotheses.

The advantages of methods in which subjects themselves are the source of information are obvious: The subject is often the only one who is able to provide the desired information (opinions, attitudes). Also, the subject speaks from personal experience. Moreover, these techniques, particularly if they have a structured form, provide reasonably reliable and objective data. Tests and scales, as well as questionnaires can achieve a high degree of methodological refinement. The strength of unstructured methods lies in the abundance of ideas and suggestions they yield. These methods prove especially useful in studies in which that abundance is of particular interest and in which the proven accuracy of an idea is not the main issue as yet (exploratory studies).

However, there are also many objections against this type of methods. The first limitation is the often encountered lack of *relevance* of data produced by the subjects themselves. Often researchers are more interested in the behaviour itself than in the subjective estimates or perceptions of this behaviour. The general weakness of the relation between attitudes and behaviour is known from literature (Guilford, 1959, ch. 9). This is also true in work and organisational psychology (see, for instance, Brayfield & Crockett, 1955; Katzell et al., 1992).

A second major problem with self-reports is the *reactivity* of these methods. By this we mean the ease and likelihood of distortion of the information through partly conscious and partly unconscious influencing by subjects themselves. In test theory, this phenomenon is known as "social desirability" (Edwards, 1959). Also, in surveys and opinion polls, especially when they concern controversial issues or topics having potentially important consequences for the subject (questions about satisfaction with pay, questions about attitudes towards lay off of personnel) an uncritical approach in which answers as such are taken too seriously will usually lead to useless results: in most cases the subject produces reactions that safeguard his or her work or employment situation, or answers randomly. This phenomenon is also well known in cross-cultural research. In Asian countries, for instance, there is a strong tendency to please or to agree with an interviewer (who is regarded as an authority). This phenomenon is known as the "courtesy bias" (Elder, 1976).

The fact that too little attention has been paid to this social desirability phenomenon has probably contributed to the negative attitude towards this type of research methods (Garfinkel, 1967; Douglas, 1976; Salancik & Pfeffer, 1977). This negative attitude is not always justified (Albinski, 1978). For the unstructured methods, such as the open interview and projection tests, this objection seems less pressing, as the intention of the researcher is not always that clear to the subject, and since the latter is also somewhat less defensive and less cautious. On the other hand, however, the reliability and validity of the information obtained with these unstructured methods is lower.

7.2   Researcher

The second category described here involves the researcher as the primary channel of information. We can again distinguish between structured methods, in which the dimensions and alternatives are selected and formulated in advance, and unstructured methods, in which this is left to the discretion of the researcher.

More *structured* methods are:

7.2.1   Systematic observation and ratings

By means of observation schedules or rating scales behaviour, process or phenomena are rec-

orded. The behaviour can take place in a natural or an artificial (for instance, a simulated) setting. The rated subjects can either be aware or unaware (one way screen) of the fact they are being observed. Furthermore, ratings can either concern intrinsic issues (for instance, the contents of discussions, Bass, 1954), or characteristics of formal processes or interactions (Bales, 1950; Andriessen et al., 1980). Sometimes, as is done in the open interview, the recording of data and the actual rating are separated in time by using a tape and/or video recorder for the registration, while the analysis of the material takes place later.

Two methods can be classified as *unstructured* methods:

7.2.2   Impressions

The researcher observes, interviews or interprets (e.g. written or drawn) material provided by the subject leading primarily to his or her own subjective impressions and conclusions, rather than focusing on a systematic analysis of the formal or content related aspects of the subject's behaviour. The researcher's personal experiences are the starting point for descriptions or predicions. This method is closely related to impressionistic or clinical rating methods in psychodiagnostics. Research findings regarding the validity of these types of impressions (Wiggins, 1972; Goldberg, 1991) make us rather reticent towards the usefulness of this source of information.

7.2.3   Participative observation

Participative observation always has to combine two potentially conflicting objectives: on the one hand sincerely participating in a process and on the other attempting to observe and evaluate this same process from a certain objective distance. The extent of participation varies from that of a fairly distant participant to participating with heart and soul. According to some (Douglas, 1976) it is best, especially when controversial or taboo topics are concerned, to start as a full participant, and, once trust has been gained, to gradually retreat into the observer role. Douglas studied controversial subjects such as nude beaches and beauty parlours in this manner.

Obviously, the method of using the "researcher

as respondent" provides a solution to the objection of reactivity of the respondent. Of course, the danger is still present. Having the observation and rating of behaviour done by a third party does not rule out the chance that the information is distorted. The subject could still influence the information in the desired direction. Furthermore, a new problem is introduced, namely, distortion of information by the researcher. Hopefully, the researcher is well-trained in unbiased observation and should have less problems with this than subjects. However, from another point of view he or she is equally not without interests (such as being overattached to certain theories or biased on basis of ideology and societal values). In addition, the reliability of the unstructured methods especially is an issue of concern. With the more structured methods reliability usually reaches acceptable levels through the use of carefully designed schemes and scales.

This concern is, however, especially for the observation methods, counterbalanced by the great advantage of *relevance*. If, for instance, employees being questioned state they have frequent contacts with others, but the observation data show that in fact there is hardly any interaction at all, it is fair to say that the subjective experience may be an interesting piece of information, but that at the same time this "observed fact", for example, in research regarding the relation between interaction and absenteeism, is more relevant than the subjective perception.

The advantages and disadvantages of objective versus participative observation have been discussed extensively (see, for instance, Zelditch, 1969; Bellack & Hersen, 1988; Köbben, 1991). These discussions focused on the choice or balance between objectivity and replicability on the one hand and relevance, validity, realistic character and avoidance of reactivity on the other. For a sober and critical evaluation, see Bouchard (1976, pp.384–392). A criterion that should not be overlooked in the use of this method is the cost in terms of personnel and time involved. It may take years of participation to reach a sufficiently high degree of acceptance; a rather large investment, which should be weighed against the quality of the information.

Lastly, the problem of selectivity of the infor-

mation should be addressed. Selectivity has been mentioned already as one of the difficulties in interviews, especially open interviews, but this objection is also relevant in observation methods. It is simply impossible to record and use everything one sees; one is forced to be selective. The question remains: to what extent does such selection introduce a strong bias?

7.3 Experts/third parties

In the third place, in data collection, one can make use of the judgement of third parties, for example, acknowledged experts or key figures.

Some of the more *structured* methods are:

7.3.1 Appraisals

Experts (personnel managers, supervisors, trainers) can assess the performance or behaviour of individuals or groups of individuals. Sometimes these ratings are readily available, for instance, in the form of performance appraisals or assessments of potential; other times they need to be designed specifically for the study in question. (For the various forms of appraising and their positive and negative sides, see Volume 3, Chapter 4 in this handbook.)

7.3.2 Interview schedules

A second possibility is to interview experts (key figures who played a crucial role in the processes to be studied) about the facts of an event and the way they experienced these. One could also use the so-called "snowball technique". One starts with an informant who played a crucial role in, for instance, a process involving a conflict of interests (such as a negotiated decision). On the basis of the first interview, a second expert (often an opponent) is selected and interviewed. This can lead to the choice of a third, and even a fourth informant. Another method used is the tracer method, in which one tries to gain insight in the historical development of a (complicated) process by identifying the phases and, for each separate phase, questioning the individuals that had an important influence on the course of the process. This can be tested against existing objective material, such as notes, minutes and agendas of meetings. For an application of these methods, see Koopman (1980), Hickson et al. (1986), and Heller et al. (1988).

Furthermore there are the *unstructured* methods. Here, of course, it is again possible to use open interviews in which the opinions of third parties are explored. Two methods deserve mentioning separately in this context. They are aimed at answering open and explorative questions about possible future developments or at generating original or uncommon solutions to given problems.

The first is the *brainstorming method* introduced by Osborn as early as 1941. The following three principles are central in the first phase of this method:

- a free flow of ideas, without paying attention to quality;
- following up on ideas introduced by others;
- a ban on criticism.

Sifting ideas on basis of quality and improving them is done at a later stage.

A second technique, that explicitly declines the use of the benefits of face-to-face interaction, is the so-called *Delphi-technique* (Helmer, 1967). This technique consists of processing individual expert opinions in the form of, for instance, an averaged score or averaged scores plus the variance in the opinions, which is then fed back to the individual participants for comments and possibly revised positioning. This process can be repeated several times. (For an example of the use of these techniques in future oriented research, see Van Doorn & Van Vught, 1978, Irvine & Martin, 1984, 1989.)

7.4   Recording/equipment

In this category no longer subjective ratings or perceptions of people, whether they are respondent, researcher or expert, are involved. The methods in this category revolve around data that can be recorded objectively. *Structured* methods are:

7.4.1   Objective indirect indicators

Due to their indirect nature, these objective measures are not easily influenced by the research subjects. These measures often belong in the category of what Webb et al. (1966) calls "unobtrusive measures". On the one hand they include physical traces such as the thumb-markedness of books or the wear of vinyl tiles in front of paintings in exhibitions as indices of their popularity, number of cigarette butts in ashtrays as an indication of the stressfulness of a meeting, etc. On the other hand they can also involve far simpler registrations, such as the place where someone sits at a conference table as a measure of dominance, the distance to (certain) others as a measure for congeniality and affinity (see Cook, 1970), etc. There is also room for this type of measures in "real life experiments" (Bovenkerk, 1978; Bovenkerk & Brunt, 1976) as is shown by a number of studies of discrimination against the Surinamese in The Netherlands. This was measured by, for instance, the relative frequency with which a seat on a streetcar next to a female Surinamese researcher remained empty (Daams, 1978), or the number of times a Surinamese researcher driving a large car was stopped for police checks as compared to a white colleague driving a similar car (Bovenkerk & Luming, 1979).

7.4.2   Experimental equipment

These instruments are mostly used in experimental research (for instance, in ergonomics). A multitude of instruments is available, either taken directly from experimental psychology (measuring heartbeat, blood pressure, skin conductance, etc.) or developed specifically for ergonomic applications (Van Wely & Willems, 1973; Sanders & McCormick, 1993; see also Sanders, Volume 2, Chapter 3 in this handbook).

Again there is the possibility to record people's behaviour and expressions directly in the form of unobtrusive measures. Equipment to record bodily movement and reactions (see Webb et al., 1966, p.152), photographic and film equipment, sometimes even using infra-red film, photo-electric cells, are all ways to analyse behaviour without the awareness of studied individuals. A good example of a complex instrument to record "locational" behaviour of people in a room is the so-called hodometer developed by Bechtel (described in Craik, 1970, p.29). It consists of a cluster of electric switch mats each independently connected to an electric counter. The entire floor area is laid whith these foot-square registers and is covered with a conceiling carpet. All steps of visitors upon the electric switch mat can be registered.

An inherent advantage of objective measurement with (often advanced) experimental equipment is that the obtained data are usually reliable. That does not mean they are valid or even less that they are relevant. Especially with the indirect registrations the advantage of a low distortion of the information is often coupled with the fault of irrelevance or invalidity. More than once the "logical distance" between the chosen measure and the studied phenomenon is so large that conclusions cannot be taken very seriously.

In addition, for many of the unobtrusive measures there is also the problem of ethical acceptability. Is it permitted to place subjects on exhibit without protecting or warning them? The dilemma is that often the very advantage of non-reactivity will force the researcher to reject this method on ethical grounds.

For the *unstructured* registration of behaviour, expressions or interactions, a variety of equipment is available to integrally record conversation, activities, events or social interaction. This information can be transcribed, coded and interpreted later. Often used for this purpose are tape recorders, film and video cameras. In principle, this method runs analogous to the interview or live observation; however, an important difference is that the audio tape, film or video tape can be replayed more than once in order to clarify obscurities or to have the material recoded to assess reliability.

7.5 Archives

Finally we want to point out a source of information that, although easily available, is often forgotten: that which has been recorded in the past. One can think of data available in personnel files or the company medical files (indications for absenteeism and turnover), or of personal or official reports, memos, agendas, notes of meetings or accounts. The latter are usually unstructured, at least they are not systematically drawn up to serve the purpose of the study, and demand careful screening and analysis. One should not forget that these documents are hardly ever written with the intention to be used in research. Furthermore, there is the problem of "selective disposing" and "selective saving", again without much concern with research interests. For an example of the use of such documentary material for an analysis of work consultation see Drenth & Koopman (1984) and for works council participation, see Koopman et al. (1981). That this category of indicators is a potentially rich source of information is witnessed from the extensive review that was dedicated to this subject by Webb et al. (1966).

From the overview presented in this section it can be concluded that there is wide array of methods available for the researcher in W&O psychology, where data collection is concerned. It will also have become clear that each of these methods has both strengths and weaknesses. Judged by the criteria of reliability and precision, validity and relevance, avoidance of reactivity, efficiency and cost, there is not one single method that will always prevail. Moreover, these criteria need to be weighed in light of the situation and topic of the study in each concrete case. It does, however, seem justified on the basis of the critical overview above to conclude that a study improves as: (a) more than one single method of research is used, and (b) more than one single instrument is used within each method. The choice would then be as much as possible in favour of a multi-method/multi-instrument approach, up to the point where costs (time, money, research subjects' patience) become prohibitive.

ACKNOWLEDGEMENTS

I wish to thank Toon Taris, Klaas Sytsma and Marise Born for their assistance with sections 5.1, 5.2 and 5.5 respectively.

REFERENCES

Aiken, L.R. (1996). *Personality and assessments: Methods and practices*. Gottingen: Hogrefe & Huber.

Albinski, M. (1978). *Onderzoek en aktie*. Assen: Van Gorcum.

Allison, P.D. (1990). Change scores as dependent variables in regression analysis. In C.C. Clogg (Ed.) *Sociological Methodology* pp.93–114. Oxford: Basil Blackwell.

Anderson, H.H., & Anderson, G.I. (Ed.) (1951). *An introduction to projective techniques*. New York: Prentice-Hall.

Andriessen, J.H.T.H., Cornelis, P., & Flier, H. van der (1980). Participatie, invloed, satisfactie en groepseffectiviteit: Een onderzoek bij deelnemers aan een bedrijfsspel. *Gedrag, 8*, 88–108.

Atkinson, J.W. (Ed.). (1958). *Motives in fantasy action, and society*. New York: Van Nostrand.

Babbie, E.R. (1979). *The practice of social research* (2nd ed.). Belmont: Wadsworth.

Bales, R.F. (1950). *Interaction process analysis*. Reading: Addison-Wesley.

Bass, B.M. (1954). The leaderless group discussion. *Psychological Bulletin, 51*, 465–492.

Bass, B.M. (1990). *Bass & Stogdill's handbook of leadership*. New York: Free Press.

Bellack, A.S., & Hersen, M. (1988). Behavioral assessment: a practical handbook (3rd ed.). New York: Pergamon Press.

Biessen, P.G.A. (1992). *Oog voor de menselijke factor*. Lisse: Swets & Zeitlinger.

Blossfeld, H.P., Hamerle, A., & Mayer, K.U. (1989). *Event history analysis: Statistical theory and application in the social sciences*. New Jersey: Lawrence Erlbaum.

Bobko, Ph. (1990). Multivariate correlational analysis. In M.D. Dunnette & L.M. Hough (Eds). *Handbook of industrial and organizational psychology* (Vol. 1, ch.11). Palo Alto, CA: Consulting Psychologists Press.

Boer, Th. de (1980). *Grondslagen van een kritische psychologie*. Baarn: Ambo.

Bosker, R.J., & Snijders, T.A.B. (1990). Statistische aspecten van multi-niveau onderzoek. *Tijdschrift voor Onderwijsresearch, 5*, 317–329. Lisse: Swets & Zeitlinger.

Bouchard, T.J. (1976). Field research methods: Interviewing, questionnaires, participant observation, systematic observation, unobtrusive measures. In M.D. Dunnette (Ed.), *Handbook of industrial and organizational psychology*. Chicago: Rand McNally.

Bovenkerk, F. (Red.) (1978). *Omdat zij anders zijn*. Meppel: Boom.

Bovenkerk, F., & Brunt, L. (1976). *Binnenste buiten en onderste boven; De anthropologie van de industrinle samenleving*. Assen: Van Gorcum.

Bovenkerk, F., & Luming, L. (1979). Surinamers en grote auto's; een levensecht experiment om rassendiscriminatie op te sporen. *Intermediair, 15*, 59–63.

Brayfield, A.D., & Crockett, W.H. (1955). Employee attitudes and employee performance. *Psychological Bulletin, 52*, 396–424.

Breakwell, G.M., Hammond, S., & Fife-Schaw, Ch. (1995). *Research methods in psychology*. London: Sage.

British Telecom (1984a). *Survey item bank: Measures of satisfaction* (Vol. 1). Bradford: MCB, University Press.

British Telecom (1984b). *Survey item bank: Measures of organizational characteristics* (Vol. 2). Bradford: MCB, University Press.

Bronfenbrenner, U. (1977). Towards an experimental ecology of human development. *American Psychologist, 32*, 513–531.

Burke, J.A., & Nesselroade, J.R. (1990). Change measurement. In A. von Eye (Red.), *Statistical methods in longitudinal research*, (pp.3–34). Boston: Academic Press.

Buros, O.K. (1978). *The eighth mental measurements yearbook* (Vol. 1 and 2). Highland Park: Gryphon Press.

Campbell, D.T. (1950). The direct assessment of social attitudes. *Psychological Bulletin*, 15–38.

Campbell, D.T., & Fiske, D.W. (1959). Convergent and discriminant validity by the multitrait-multimethod matrix. *Psychological Bulletin, 56*, 81–105.

Campbell, J.P. (1976). Psychometric theory. In M.D. Dunnette (Ed.), *Handbook of industrial and organizational psychology*. Chicago: Rand McNally.

Campbell, D.T., & Stanley, J.C. (1963). *Experimental and quasi-experimental designs for research*. Chicago: Rand McNally.

Carsten, J.M., & Spector, R. (1987). Unemployment, job satisfaction, and employee turnover. *Journal of Applied Psychology, 72*, 374–381.

Clark, P.A. (1972). *Action research and organizational change*. London: Harper & Row.

Cohen, J. (1960). A coefficient of agreement for nominal scales. *Educational and Psychological Measurement, 20*, 37–46.

Cook, M. (1970). Experiments on orientation and proxemies. *Human Relations, 23*, 61–76.

Cook, Th.D., & Campbell, D.T. (1976). The design and conduct of quasi-experiments and true experiments in field setting. In M.D. Dunnette (Ed.), *Handbook of industrial and organizational psychology*. Chicago: Rand McNally.

Cook, Th.D., & Campbell, D.T. (1979). *Quasi-experimentation: design and analysis issues for field settings*. Chicago: Rand McNally.

Cook, Th.D., Campbell, D.T., & Peracchio, L. (1990). Quasi Experimentation. In M.D. Dunnette & Hough, L.M. (Eds), *Handbook of industrial and organizational psychology* (Vol. 1, ch.9). Palo Alto, CA: Consulting Psychologists Press.

COP (1959). *Bazen in de industrie*. Den Haag: COP.

Cox, R.D. (1972). Regression models and life tables (with discussion). *Journal of the Royal Statistical Society*, Series B, *34*, 187–220.

Cozijnsen, A.J., & Vrakking, W. (1993). *Handbook of innovation management*. Oxford: Blackwell.

Craik, H.K. (1970). Environmental Psychology. In H.C. Craik (Ed.), *New directions in psychology*. New York: Holt, Rinehart & Winston.

Cronbach, L.J. (1990). *Essentials of psychological testing*. New York: Harper.

Cronbach, L.J., & Suppes, P. (1969). *Research for tomorrow schools: Disciplined inquiry for education*. New York.

Cronbach, L.J., & Furby, L. (1970). How to measure "change"—or should we? *Psychological Bulletin, 74*, 68–80.

Daams, M.C. (1978). Naast wie zal ik nu eens gaan zitten? In Bovenkerk, F. (Red.), *Omdat zij anders zijn*. Assen: Boom.

Doorn, J. van, & Vught, F. van (1978). *Forecasting*. Assen: Van Gorcum & Comp.

Douglas, J.D. (1976). *Investigative social research*. Beverly Hills: Sage.

Drenth, P.J.D. (1960). *Een onderzoek naar de motieven bij het kiezen van een beroep* (diss.). Amsterdam: Van Soest.

Drenth, P.J.D. (1988). De waarde van het selectie-interview. *Gedrag en Organische, 2*, 18–26.

Drenth, P.J.D. (1994). Scientific and social responsibility: A dilemma for the psychologist as a scientist? *European Work and Organizational Psychologist, 3*, 45–57.

Drenth, P.J.D., & Koopman, P.L. (1984). A contingency approach to participative leadership: how good? In J.G. Hunt, D.M. Hosking, C.A. Schriesheim, & R. Stewart (Eds), *Leaders and managers: International perspectives on managerial behavior and leadership*. New York: Pergamon.

Drenth, P.J.D., & Koopman, P.L. (1984). Experience with "werkoverleg" in The Netherlands implications for quality circles. *Journal of General Management, 9*, 57–73.

Drenth, P.J.D., & Sijtsma, K. (1990). *Testtheorie*. Houten: Bohn Stafleu Van Loghum.

Durlak, J.A., & Lipsey, M.W. (1991). A practitioner's guide to meta-analysis. *American Journal of Community Psychology, 19*, 291–332.

Edwards, A.L. (1959). Social desirability and personality test construction. In I.A. Berg and B.M. Bass, *Cognitive approaches to personality measurements*. New York: McGraw-Hill.

Edwards, A.L. (1965). *Experimental design in psychological research*. New York: Holt, Rinehart & Winston.

Eeden, P. van den, & Meijnen, G.W. (1990). Onderwijsonderzoek vanuit multi-niveau perspectief. *Tijdschrift voor Onderwijsresearch, 5*, 259–272. Lisse: Swets & Zeitlinger.

Elder, J.W. (1976). Comparative cross-national methodology. *Annual Review of Sociology, 2*, 209–230.

Elshout-Mohr, J.J., Elshout, M., & Wijngaart, J. van de (1967). *Hinrarchische clusteranalyse uitgaande van een intercorrelatiematrix*. Amsterdam: ICO, Universiteit van Amsterdam.

Elster, J. (1983). *Explaining technical change*. Cambridge: Cambridge University Press.

Engel, J.F., Kollat, D.J., & Blackwell, R.D. (1968). *Consumer behavior*. New York: Holt, Rinehart & Winston.

European Commission (1994). *The European Report on Science and Technology Indicators*. Brussels: ECSC-EC-EAEC.

Evers, A., Vliet-Mulder, J.C. van, & Ter Laak, J. (1992). *Documentatie van Tests en Testresearch in Nederland*. Amsterdam: N. I. P.

Flippo, E.B. (1971). *Principles of personnel administration*. New York: McGraw-Hill.

Frank, L.L., & Hackman, J.R. (1975). Effects of interviewer interviewee similarity on interviewer objectivity in college admission interviews. *Journal of Applied Psychology, 60*, 366–368.

Freedman, J.L. (1969). Role playing: Psychology by consensus. *Journal of Personality and Social Psychology, 13*, 107–114.

Fromkin, H.L. & Streufert, S. (1976). Laboratory experimentation. In M.D. Dunnette (Ed.), *Handbook of industrial and organizational psychology*. Chicago: Rand McNally.

Gagné, R.M. (1962). Simulators. In R. Glaser (Ed.), *Training, research and education*. New York: Wiley.

Garfinkel, H. (1967). *Studies in ethno-methodology*. Engelwood Cliffs: Prentice-Hall.

Ghiselli, E.E., Campbell, J.P., & Zedek, S. (1981). *Measurement theory for the behavioral sciences*. San Francisco: Freeman & Comp.

Glass, G.V. (1976). Primary, secondary and meta-analysis of research. *Educational Researcher, 10*, 3–8.

Goldberg, L.R. (1991). Human mind versus regression equation: Five contrasts. In D. Cichetti & W.M. Grove (Eds.), *Thinking clearly about psychology* (Vol. 1). Minneapolis: University of Minneapolis Press.

Goldman, L. (1961). *Using tests in counseling*. New York: Harper.

Goodman, S.N. (1991). Have you ever meta-analysis you didn't like? *Annals of Internal Medicine, 114*, 244–246.

Groot, A.D. de (1961). *Methodologie; grondslagen van denken en onderzoeken in de gedragswetenschappen*. Den Haag: Mouton.

Groot, A.D. de (1971). *Een minimale methodologie*. Den Haag: Mouton.

Groot, A.D. de (1990). Forumbegrip en forumtheorie. In F.P.H. Dijksterhuis, & J. Griffiths (Eds), *De Forum-theorie bij de sociaal-wetenschappelijke bestudering van het recht*. Groningen: Wolters-Noordhoff.

Guilford, J.P. (1959). *Personality*. New York: McGraw-Hill.

Guion, R.M. (1990). Personnel assessment, selection and placement. In M.D. Dunnette, & L.M. Hough (Eds), *Handbook of industrial and organizational psychology* (Vol. 2, ch.6). Palo Alto, CA: Consulting Psychologists Press.

Hagenaars, J.A. (1990). *Categorical longitudinal data: Log-linear panel, trend, and cohort analysis.* Newbury Park, CA: Sage.

Hamakers, J.A.P. (1990). *Idolen van een methodoloog; over causaal verklaren in de sociale wetenschappen.* Tilburg: Tilburg University Press.

Handel, W. (1982). *Ethno-methodology; how people make sense.* Englewood Cliffs: Prentice Hall.

Hays, W.L. (1963). *Statistics for psychologists.* New York: Holt, Rinehart & Winston.

Hedges, L.V., & Olkin, I. (1985). *Statistical methods for meta-analysis.* Orlando, FL: Academic Press.

Heller, F.A. (1960). Group feedback analysis: A method of field research. *Psychological Bulletin, 72,* 108–117.

Heller, F.A. (1970). Group feedback analysis a change agent. *Human Relations, 23,* 319–333.

Heller, F.A. (1976). Group feedback analysis as a method of action research. In A.W. Clark (Ed.), *Experience in action research.* New York: Plenum Press.

Heller, F.A., Drenth, P.J.D., Koopman, P.L., & Rus, V. (1988). *Decisions in organizations; a three country comparative study.* London: Sage.

Helmer, O. (1967). *Analysis of the future: the delphi method.* Santa Monica, CA: Rand Corp.

Hermans, H.J.M. (1988). On the integration of nomothetic and idiographic research methods in the study of personal meaning. *Journal of Personality, 56,* 785–812.

Herriot, P. (Ed.) (1989). *Assessment and selection in organizations.* Chichester: Wiley.

Hickson, D.J., Butler, R.J., Cray, D., Mallory, G.R., & Wilson, D.C. (1986). *Top decisions: strategic decision-making in organizations.* Oxford: Basil Blackwell.

Hofstede, G.H. (1967). *The game of budget control.* Assen: Van Gorcum & Comp.

Hofstede, G.H. (1980). *Culture's consequences.* London: Sage.

Hofstee, W.K.B. (1975). De betrekkelijkheid van sociaal wetenschappelijke uitspraken. *Nederlands Tijdschrift voor de Psychologie, 30,* 373–600.

Huizinga, J. (1986). *Herfsttij der middeleeuwen.* Groningen: Wolters Noordhoff, 20ste druk.

Hulin, Ch. (1990). Adaptation, persistence and commitment in organizations. In M.D. Dunnette, & L.M. Hough (Eds), *Handbook of industrial and organizational psychology.* (Vol. 2, ch.8). Palo Alto, CA: Consulting Psychologists Press.

Hunter, J.E., & Schmidt, F.L. (1990). *Methods of meta-analyis: correcting error and bias in research findings.* Newbury Park, CA: Sage.

Hunter, J.E., & Schmidt, F.L. (1991). Meta-analysis. In R.K. Hambleton & J.N. Zaal (Red.), *Advances in educational and psychological testing: theory and applications.* Boston/Dordrecht: Kluwer.

Iaffaldano, M., & Muchinsky, P. (1985). Job selection and job performance: A meta-analysis. *Psychological Bulletin, 97,* 251–273.

IDE International Research Group (1981a). *Industrial democracy in Europe.* Oxford: Oxford University Press.

IDE International Research Group (1981b). *Industrial relations.* Oxford: Oxford University Press.

IDE International Research Group (1993). *Industrial democracy in Europe revisited.* Oxford: Oxford University Press.

Irvine, J., & Martin, B.R. (1984). *Foresight in science: Picking the winners.* London: Pinter Publ.

Irvine, J., & Martin, B.R. (1989). *Research foresight: creating the future.* Den Haag: Neth. Min. Ed. & Science.

Janis, I.L. (1982). *Victims of group think.* Boston: Houghton Mifflin.

Kahn, R.L., & Cannell, C.F. (1957). *The dynamics of interviewing.* New York: Wiley.

Katona, G. (1960). *The powerful consumer.* New York: McGraw-Hill.

Katzell, R.A., Thomson, D.E., & Guzzo, R.A. (1992). How job satisfaction and job performance are and are not linked. In C.J. Crannig, P.E. Smith, & E.F. Stone (Eds), *Job satisfaction.* New York: Lexington Books.

Keppel, G. (1991). Design and analysis. New York: Prentice Hall.

Kerlinger, F.N. (1973). Foundations of behavioral research. New York: Holt Rinehart & Winston.

Kessler, R.C., & Greenberg, D.F. (1981). *Linear panel analysis: Models of quantitative change.* London: Academic Press.

Klein, S.M., Kraut, A.J., & Wolfson, A. (1971). Employee reactions to attitude survey feedback. *Administrative Science Quarterly, 16,* 497–514.

Köbben, A.J.F. (1977). Participerende oservatie, ja! Maar hoe en waartoe? *Amsterdams Sociologisch Tijdschrift, 3,* 301–310.

Köbben, A.J.F. (1991). *De weerbarstige waarheid.* Amsterdam: Prometheus.

Koopman, P.L. (1980). *Besluitvorming in organisaties.* Assen: Van Gorcum.

Koopman, P.L., Drenth, P.J.D., Bus, F.B., Kruyswijk, A.J., & Wierdsma, A.F. (1981). Context, process and effects of participative decision making on the shop floor: three cases in the Netherlands. *Human Relations, 34,* 675–676.

Kühn, Th. (1962). *The structure of scientific revolutions.* Chicago: Chicago University Press.

Lawlis, G.F., & Lu, E. (1972). Judgment of counseling process. Reliability agreement and error. *Psychological Bulletin, 78,* 17–20.

Lewin, K. (1946). Action research and minority problems. *The Journal of Social Issues, 2,* 34–36.

Locke, E.A. (1986). *Generalizing from laboratory to field settings.* New York: Lexington Books.

Lonner, W.J., & Berry, J.W. (1986) (Eds). *Field methods in cross cultural research*. Beverly Hills: Sage.

Luthans, F. (1992). Organizational behavior (6th ed.). New York: McGraw-Hill.

Mayfield, E.C. (1964). The selection interview: A review of research. *Personnel Psychology, 17*, 239–260.

Mann, F.C. (1957). Studying and creating chance: A means to understanding social organization. Research in industrial human relations: A critical appraisal. New York: Harper, pp.146–167.

Maslow, A.H. (1954). *Motivation and personality*. New York: Harper.

McClelland, D.C. (1961). *The achieving society*. Princeton: Van Nostrand.

Meerling, (1980). *Methoden en technieken van psychologisch onderzoek* (Deel 1 en 2). Meppel/Amsterdam: Boom.

MMW (Ministerie van Maarschappelijk Werk) (1960). *What is community self-survey*. Den Haag: MMW.

Mulder, M. (1977). *Omgaan met macht*. Amsterdam: Elsevier.

Nunnally, J.C. (1967). *Psychometric theory*. New York: McGraw-Hill.

Oppenheim, A.W. (1966). *Questionnaire design and attitude measurement*. London: Heinemann.

Osborn, A.F. (1941). *Applied imagination: Principles and procedures of creative thinking*. New York: Harper & Row.

Petersen, D.R. (1995). The reflective educator. *American Psychologist, 50*, 975–983.

Petty, M.M., McGee, G.W., & Cavender, J.W. (1984). A meta-analysis of the relationships between individual job satisfaction and individual performance. *Academy of Management Review, 9*, 712–721.

Phillips, D.L. (1973). *Abandoning method*. Jossey-Bass.

Popper, K.R. (1959). *The logic of scientific discovery*. London: Hutchinson.

Popping, R. (1983). *Overeenstemmingsmaten voor nominale data*. Universiteit van Groningen, dissertation.

Price, J.L. (1972). *Handbook of organizational measurement*. Lexington, MA: Heath.

Pugh, D.S., Hickson, Hinings, C.R., & Turner, C. (1968). Dimensions of organization structure. *Administrative Science Quarterly, 13*, 65–105.

Randell, G. (1978). Interviewing at work. In P.B. Warr, *Psychology at work* (2nd ed.). London: Penguin.

Richardson, S.A., Dohrenwend, B.S. & Klein, D. (1965). *Interviewing*. New York: Basic Books.

Rosenthal, R., & Rosnov, R. (1991). *Meta-Analytic procedures for social research* (2nd ed.). Beverly Hills, CA: Sage.

Runkel, Ph.J., & McGrath, J.E. (1972). *Research on human behaviour*. New York: Holt, Rinehart & Winston.

Sackett & Larson, J.R. (1990). Research strategics and tactics in industrial and organizational psychology. In M.D. Dunnette, & L.M. Hough (Eds). *Handbook of industrial and organizational psychology* (Vol. 1, ch.8). Palo Alto, CA: Consulting Psychologists Press.

Salancik, G.R., & Pfeffer, J.P. (1977). An examination of need-satisfaction models of job attitudes. *Administrative Science Quarterly, 22*, 427–456.

Sandefur, G.D., & Tuma, N.B. (1987). How data type affects conclusions about individual mobility. *Social Science Research, 16*, 301–328.

Sanders, M.S., & McCormick, E.J. (1993). *Human factors in engineering and design*. New York: McGraw-Hill.

Saunders, D.R. (1956). Models variables in prediction. *Educational and Psychological Measurement, 16*, 209–222.

Schmidt, N. (1976). Social and situation determinants of interview decisions: Implications for the employment interview. *Personnel Psychology, 29*, 79–101.

Schön, D.A. (1987). *Educating the reflective practitioner: how professionals think in actions*. San Francisco: Jossey-Bass.

Schwarzer, R. (1989). *Meta-analysis programs manual*. Freie Universität, Institut für Psychologie.

Seashore, S., & Bowers, D.G. (1964). *Changing the structure and the functioning of an organization*. Ann Arbor: Survey Research Center.

Shrout, P.E., & Fleiss, J.L. (1979). Intraclass correlations: uses in assessing rater reliability. *Psychological Bulletin, 86*, 420–428.

Sims, D., Fineman, S., & Gabriel, Y. (1993). *Organizing & organizations*. London: Sage.

Smith, G.H. (1954). *Motivation research in advertising and marketing*. New York: McGraw-Hill.

Smith, P.C., Kendall, L.M., & Hulin, C.L. (1969). *The measurement of satisfaction in work and retirement*. Chicago: Rand McNally.

Strien, P.J. van (1975). Naar een methodologie van het praktijk denken in de sociale wetenschappen. *Nederlands Tijdschrift voor de Psychologie, 30*, 601–619.

Strien, P.J. van (1978). *Om de kwaliteit van het bestaan*. Meppel: Boom.

Susman, G.I., & Evered, R.D. (1978). An assessment of the scientific merits of action research. *Administrative Science Quarterly, 23*, 582–603.

Taris, A.W. (1994). *Analysis of career data from a life-course perspective*. Amsterdam: Vrije Universiteit, Academisch proefschrift.

Tinsley, H.E.A., & Weiss, D.J. (1975). Interrates reliability and agreement of subjective judgments. *Journal of Counseling Psychology, 22*, 358–376.

Ven, A.H. van der, & Ferry, D.L. (1980). *Measuring and assessing organizations*. New York: Wiley.

Wanouw, J.P., Sullivan, S.E., & Malinak, J. (1989). The role of judgement calls in meta-analysis. *Journal of Applied Psychology, 74*, 259–264.

Wardekker, W. (1978), Actieonderzoek in de onderwij-smethode. *Kennis en Methode*, *1*, 44–55.

Webb, E.J., Campbell, D.T., Schwartz, R.C., & Sechrest, L. (1966). *Unobtrusive measures*. Chicago: Rand McNally.

Wely, P.W. van, & Willems, P.J. (1973). *Ergonomie: mens en werk*. Deventer: Kluwer.

Whyte, W.F. (1960). Interviewing in fieldresearch. In R.N. Adams, & Preiss, J.J. (Ed.), *Human organizations research*. Homewood: Dorsey.

Wiggins, J.S. (1972). *Personality and prediction*. Reading: Addison-Wesley.

Wolff, F.M. (1986). *Meta-Analysis*. Beverly Hills, CA: Sage.

Wolff-Albers, A.D. (1968). *Een poging tot evaluatie van een tertiaire-opleiding, of het nut van controle groepen*. Groningen: Wolters-Noordhoff.

Zeegers, F.E. (1989). Het meten van overeenstemming. *Nederlands Tijdschrift voor de Psychologie*, *44*, 145–156.

Zelditch, M. (1969). Some methodological problems of field studies. In G.J. McGall, & R.G. Simmons (Eds), *Issues in participant observations*. Reading: Addison-Wesley.

3

The Role of the Work and Organizational Psychologist

Charles J. de Wolff

1 INTRODUCTION

In 1974 Wolfle, the director of the American Psychological Association wrote in his yearly report: "The central fact of psychology today is the rapidity of growth" (Wolfle, 1947). Wolfle had reason to be proud; membership of the APA had grown that year from 4500 to 5100. When the APA was founded in 1892 there were just 32 members. Also today rapidity of growth remains a central fact. At the centennial in 1992 the APA had about 75,000 members; in 1995 there were 83,498 members and 57,375 affiliates. (Report of the treasurer, Koocher, 1996).

Rapid growth has not only occurred in the USA. At the beginning of the century there were at most a few hundred psychologists. In 1992 Rosenzweig estimated the number of psychologists in the world to be 500,000 (Rosenzweig, 1992) but outside the USA the rapid growth was seen to start later. The figures for The Netherlands back this up. In 1947 there were 60 psychologists; in 1970, 2100; in 1990, 18,000; in 1996, 23,000. The expectation is that there will be 30,000 psychol-

ogists in 2005 (Ministerie van Onderwijs en Wetenschappen, 1995). This means that in time 1 in every 500 Dutchmen will be a psychologist!

Rapidity of growth is also reflected in the number of psychology students. In 1992 there were 9946 psychology students in The Netherlands, of whom 2124 were enrolled in the first year. This means that 1 in every 1600 Dutchmen was a psychology student. Also other European countries have reported rapid growth. Prieto (1991) reports that in 1984–1985 there were 27,245 psychology students in Spain. In 1989–1990 this had increased to 44,110.

Half a million psychologists is an impressive number. Rosenzweig compares this with the number of physicians, which is estimated to be one million. *The Economist* (18 July 1992) published data about lawyers. Worldwide there are about two million. There are however substantial differences between countries. The USA and some Asian countries have relatively large numbers of lawyers, while in a number of European countries the number of psychologists is greater than the number of physicians or lawyers.

There is also growth to be seen in other social sciences. It is estimated that in 2005 in The

Netherlands there will be 120,000 social scientists (of whom 30,000 will be psychologists). It appears that psychology is growing more rapidly than other social sciences like sociology and pedagogy.

When one makes comparisons definitions are important. In most statistics figures are presented on university graduates. In other statistics data are given about membership of associations or the number of people active in a particular field. One should be careful about drawing conclusions from comparisons.

Nevertheless the figures show that psychology is growing rapidly. Goodstein (1988) quotes Hilgard, who jokingly remarked in the fifties that the world population was growing by 1% a year, but the population of psychologists by 10% a year. Extrapolation leads to the conclusion that by 2100 the number of psychologists will be larger than the world population!

The remarkable fact is that now, some 40 years on psychology is still rapidly growing. What consequences does this have for psychology and for the roles that psychologists play in society?

Psychology is a discipline with many specialties and sub-specialties. At the beginning of the century this was not the case. Psychologists advertised themselves as generalists and general psychologists. They were active in different fields of application. In some countries like Indonesia, universities are reluctant to introduce specializations into the training programme. Students are required to study different fields of application like clinical, and work and organizational (W&O) psychology. In that way they are supposed to have a better chance in the labour market.

In most countries, however, universities have introduced specialization. Students are required to select a particular field or subject, usually after completing a general introduction programme to psychology.

One particular field is work and organizational psychology. The growth of this specialty has proved to be different from other specialties. (Krijnen, 1975, 1976, Holtzer, 1984, Van Drunen & Breyer, 1994). This difference has been well-documented for The Netherlands. Until the early sixties the growth of W&O psychology was more or less the same as for psychology in general. But in the latter part of the sixties growth started to lag. Students were reluctant to choose this field of specialization preferring clinical, social and developmental psychology. In society in general industrial organizations were not popular; psychologists working in such organizations were often depicted as "lackeys of management" (see for an analysis of this period, Van Strien, 1978a, b).

The stagnation in growth was serious. A study done in collaboration with the Dutch Psychological Association (NIP) predicted the percentage of W&O psychologists would decrease from 13% in the early sixties to 2.4% in 1984 (Krijnen, 1976). The actual course of development proved different as in the latter part of the seventies, interest in W&O psychology had started to increase. After 1980 growth became exponential. Interest in clinical and developmental psychology decreased and a rapid growth in interest was seen among students for W&O psychology.

Some statistics gathered from other countries show similar trends. In Germany there were 300 members of the Association of W&O psychology in 1960. In 1970 there were 400; in 1980 there were 800; in 1990, 3000 (Winterfeld, 1992). A Spanish study showed that 16.3% of all psychologists were W&O psychologists. (Diaz & Quintanilla, 1992, Peiro & Munduate 1994). A Mexican study (Urbino & Hidalgo, 1992) shows that of 739 graduate students, 9% selected W&O psychology.

The situation in the USA took a different course. In 1981 7.5% of APA members were I&O psychologists (Howard et al., 1986) but the percentage of PhD recipients was only 3% in 1971 and 4% in 1991 (Pion et al., 1996). That the percentage of I&O psychology members in the APA is bigger has to do with certain shifts. Graduates in other specialties, especially in personality, social and experimental psychology, find employment in business, government and other organizations (Howard et al., 1986). So here the increase as a consequence does not primarily stem from changes in the choice of specialty during study but rather from shifts in employment after graduation.

When looking at all the different studies a good guess would be that 10% of all psychologists are

FIGURE 3.1

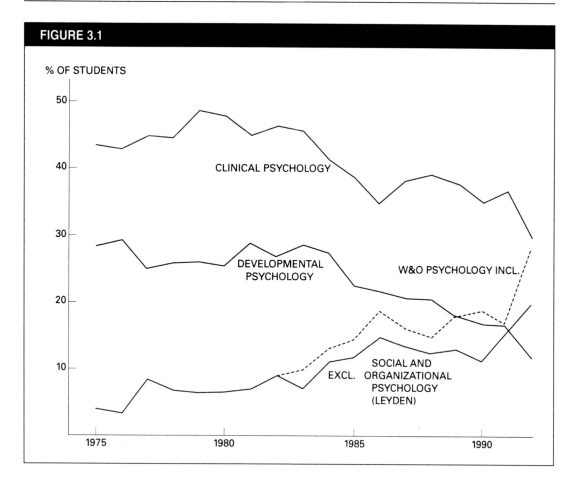

% OF STUDENTS

CLINICAL PSYCHOLOGY

DEVELOPMENTAL
PSYCHOLOGY

W&O PSYCHOLOGY INCL.

EXCL.

SOCIAL AND
ORGANIZATIONAL
PSYCHOLOGY
(LEYDEN)

Choice of specialization in the Psychology Study Programme in The Netherlands (1975–1992).

W&O psychologists. This is a rough estimate but it would mean that worldwide there are 50,000 W&O psychologists. Taking into account the observed rapid increase in W&O students, this figure is set to grow rapidly. Therefore Wolfle's statement also applies to this field. And also here the big question is what the consequences will be for the roles W&O psychologists fulfil in society.

There is yet another shift. Particularly during the eighties the number of female students selecting W&O psychology increased considerably. Pion reports that in 1971 6% of the I&O PhD recipients were female, in 1991 this was 53%. Also in Europe there has been a sharp increase in the number of female psychologists. A few decades ago W&O psychology was mainly selected by male students. However, in recent years the majority of students have been female.

Not all psychologists graduating from university find employment within a reasonable amount of time. In The Netherlands, unemployment among psychologists was not a serious problem until the early seventies. However in the latter part of the seventies and during the eighties unemployment increased rapidly. In 1983 there were 1500 unemployed psychologists which was about 13% of the total number of psychologists and was equivalent to twice the number of psychologists graduating per year. The number grew to about 2000 at the end of the eighties, and has decreased somewhat in the nineties (Ministerie van Onderwijs en Wetenschappen, 1995). Unemployment is a very serious problem for the clinical psychologist but also for social and developmental psychologists. On the one hand this has to do with the limited demand, but on the other hand there are large numbers of students selecting these specialties (see also Figure 3.1). Many clinical psychologists have not managed to find employment for periods of over a year. Graduates often feel obliged to accept jobs which show little or no correspondence with their training programme.

The situation is more favourable for W&O psychologists. Most graduates, at least in The Netherlands, succeed in finding a job within a few months of graduation (Holzer, 1984 Nijsten, 1984, de Greef, 1993). They find jobs in universities, industrial firms, consultancy agencies or service organizations.

Unemployment of psychologists is much less of a problem in the USA. Howard mentioned in 1986 that unemployment rates for all psychologists and for new PhD recipients have hovered around 2% (Howard et al., 1986). These rates are favourable compared with those for other scientific and engineering fields. Also Pion (1996) reports low unemployment rates for psychology PhDs: in 1991 0.9% for men and 1.7% for women (unemployed and seeking work). Striking is that health service providers, the majority of PhDs, do better than all other subfields combined. So the USA does not experience the problem of clinical psychologists failing to find jobs.

W&O psychologists fulfil roles in society (Sardin & Allen, 1969, Katz & Kahn, 1978). This means that they not only perform certain duties but also that they themselves and the people with whom they collaborate have certain ideas about how a person should behave in a certain position. The focal person has ideas about his/her conduct, and the members of the role set have expectations as to how someone should behave in certain situations. Roles have to do with views and expectations, about rights and obligations and rewards. They are closely related to the way one defines reality, and how one perceives his/her own position.

Katz and Kahn point out that there is continuous interaction between a person who fulfils a role (the focal person) and his/her social environment (the role senders). In such interactions opinions, beliefs and expectations about one another are shaped. Role senders can send opinions which are incompatible with those of other role senders or those of the focal person. This creates role conflict.

They can also send ambiguous information which creates role ambiguity. Yet it is in such interaction processes that roles are shaped and accommodated to new developments. Roles are not static. It is within the continuous process of interaction that roles are developed and adapted.

Roles have an individual and collective aspect. The interactive processes have to do with a particular individual in a particular position and lead to the definition of that person's role. But there are also collective aspects, e.g when a person is a member of a profession such a person is not only seen as an individual but also as a representative of that profession. Not only a focal person but also his/her social environment, hold views on how professionals should behave and what they can expect from their social environment. In society in general there are opinions, beliefs and expectations held about W&O psychologists. Such opinions are held not only by W&O psychologists, but also by the role senders. Opinions have to do with the tasks W&O psychologists perform, and the way they interact with clients. Again these opinions are not static. During continuous interactive processes these opinions are shaped and adapted.

Part of the collective opinions are codified. Professional associations have made rules which prescribe how psychologists should act in particular situations. In this way important aspects of the role of the psychologist are defined. This does not mean however that all aspects are defined. A code of conduct is meant to regulate the behaviour of the members of the profession; it also points out what in potential conflict situations the rights and the obligations are of the professionals but also of their clients and other parties. This enables arbitration of conflicts. Parties who feel themselves to be treated unfairly can file complaints. Associations have appointed special committees to handle such complaints.

Roles however possess more aspects than are covered in the code of conduct. Important aspects are those which have to do with the domain of the profession and the relationship with the client.

This chapter is about the role of the W&O psychologist. How do W&O psychologists perceive themselves, what are their duties and how are they perceived by their role senders. The rapid growth by the profession is an important aspect in this respect. Growth does not only mean more of the same. Growth usually implies structural changes. When the number of W&O psychologists increases one may expect that this will have consequences regarding the roles they play in society. The history of the subject provides us with plenty of examples (see e.g. Volume 1, Chapter 4 of this *Handbook*). Professions develop. One can distinguish stages, each with its own challenges and opportunities. At the beginning of the century W&O psychology was a field with only a small number of pioneers who were very active and had visionary ideas about what W&O psychology could mean to society. One of their most pressing problems was to get the subject as such accepted in society, particularly in universities. Schönpflug (1993) gives a vivid account of the problems and particularly how difficult it was to get cooperation from philosophers in order to establish chairs in psychology.

The problems experienced in the middle of the century were completely different ones. At that time it was important to enlarge the knowledge base of the subject and to build research departments.

Now at the end of the century the situation has changed once again. The number of professionals is high and the knowledge base substantial. Rosenzweig (1992) estimates that 15% of psychologists are involved in research. Every year thousands of publications appear. What consequences does this have for the role of the W&O psychologists?

The word psychologist is used in two ways. It defines a person who has completed a particular training programme. In several countries such people are given the title: "psychologist". However it has an additional meaning: someone who practices a particular profession. The two are not the same. Some individuals who have been trained as psychologists decide to take up other professions. For example they become personnel officers or organizational consultants. They qualify as psychologists but then go on to practise something different. In this chapter both categories will be dealt with.

In this chapter the professionalization process

will be looked at, after which the domain of the W&O psychologist will be discussed and the W&O psychologist's client. Next there will be discussion on the training of W&O psychologists, the professional association, the relationship with other professions and the relationship with the government. At the end of this chapter the future of W&O psychology is considered. It is not the intention to predict, but rather to analyse and to understand. A distinct characteristic of a profession is that members of the profession set goals for themselves. Members adhere to values and strive for vindication of such values. De Groot (1971) always stressed the importance of the scientific forum for the development of psychology. Also within a profession there is a forum of professionals, which reflect on the development of the subject; and which wants to direct the subject in a particular way. The analyses in this chapter are meant to be a contribution to the discussion in this forum.

An author writing about the psychologist's role should be aware of cultural differences and differences in social economic systems. In scientific studies such differences do not usually play a major role. Yet roles have to do with norms and values, so role interpretation can differ from one country to another. Laws, i.e. law interpretation and law enforcement in different countries, are not the same. There are many examples where this has an impact on the psychologist's role. For example psychologists in personnel selection in the USA have to work with the extensive regulations on equal opportunity. This has had consequences for selection procedures which have often been subject to scrutiny in court sessions and had to be defended in litigation processes. That is a very different situation from the one usually found in European countries.

There has been very little research done on the role of psychologists in different countries. The author of this chapter is a Dutch psychologist whose norms and values have been shaped by Dutch society. Despite experience gained as an officer of an international psychological association, it certainly does not make one an expert in cultural differences. Nevertheless he is convinced that there are at present developments in the profession which merit attention and since probably no one is completely familiar with differences in roles, it does make sense to attempt to make an analysis of such developments, even with limited experience.

2   THE PROFESSION OF PSYCHOLOGIST

For individuals, offering their services to clients, it is attractive to become a member of a profession. As a member of a profession one can profit from the behavioural patterns, opinions and expectations which have been formed in the past. Any individual, confronted with a health problem, knows how to go about consulting a physician. They have developed what Schank and Abelson call "scripts". (Abelson, 1981; Wegman, 1985) this being how to consult one's general practitioner. Due to such scripts they know how to find a general practitioner, even when they are not in familiar surroundings; they know how to expect their practitioner to behave, e.g. in using a stethoscope and prescribing drugs. Such scripts facilitate the access to and the interaction with the professional; they are highly helpful, both for the practitioner and the client. A service provider who is not able to make use of such a script has to invest an enormous amount of effort in contacting clients and explaining the nature of the services he/she has to offer. Clients using a script might never have seen the service provider before, whereas he/she still has a good idea about what to expect.

For the medical profession there are well-developed scripts; for most other professions scripts have been developed to a lesser extent. Either the number of clients who are familiar with the service provider is smaller or the clients know less about the service provider. For W&O psychologists there are clients who possess extensive experience, e.g. for personnel selection and training but there are many clients who have none at all. But even when the usefulness is more limited it can still be very attractive for someone providing personnel selection services to advertise himself or herself as a W&O psychologist.

Another reason for the attraction of being a member of a profession is the recognition it brings. Some services may only be carried out by recognized professionals. Access to clients is restricted to those who are recognized either by law, or by the profession. Employers may require that applicants be a member of a profession. The membership of a profession can also provide necessary prestige to individuals.

2.1   Colleague surveillance

While it can be profitable to belong to a profession one also has to pay a price. The profession guarantees, implicitly or explicitly, that their members will serve clients well and this implies a degree of surveillance. A service provider who does not behave in accordance with the values of the profession damages the interests of the said profession.

Professions usually have a code of conduct, and explicit rules as to how members should behave in certain situations. Clients who feel that a professional person has not observed such rules can file complaints. There is usually a special committee dealing with such complaints. The most severe sanction is being expelled from membership and losing the right to practise.

There are other forms of surveillance which are less formal. Colleagues are important role senders. There are many ways to let colleagues know how they are expected to behave and to appeal to a person's adherence to norms and values which are considered to be of importance to the profession. Those who behave well and contribute to the profession might be invited to take up positions in the profession and will gain prestige and influence. Those who are seen as not acting in accordance with the values might be excluded from such positions.

So being a member of a profession has its benefits, but also its price. Furthermore professional associations usually impose a substantial fee. This might discourage individuals from becoming a member. Such is the case for many young W&O psychologists who have found employment in organizations where gaining access to clients does not form a major problem for them. Here they might perceive it themselves as being a psychologist without the need for becoming a member of a professional association. This loosens the ties with the profession and it may even occur that such ties are broken. An example could be a person who has graduated in psychology but decided to advertise himself as an organizational consultant or a personnel officer.

Therefore the decision to become a member of a profession is very much a matter of weighing up the costs against the benefits. The benefits provide the access to clients, recognition, support from colleagues and prestige while the costs involve being subjected to colleague surveillance and the membership fee.

2.2 The establishment of the profession

One can only be a member of a profession if there is a profession but how do professions come into being? Sociologists have studied this and published books on this subject, particularly during the sixties. Mok (1973) summarizes this literature and describes three stages.

The first stage is the one of *differentiation*. It starts when there is a need in society for a particular type of expert who can solve particular problems. In a complex society new problems always arise, so a demand for new expertise is created. An example of this is the new Dutch ARBO law. It has been observed that there are all kinds of problems regarding health, safety and well-being in organizations and as a consequence the number of disabled workers is increasing. The government wants to stimulate prevention and is obliging organizations to make use of qualified experts, such as industrial physicians, ergonomists and work and organization experts. And so a demand has been created for ARBO experts. According to the theory one may expect that such experts would interact and create mutual solutions for the kind of problems they encounter. Through joint activities the process of professionalization does get started.

The next stage is *institutionalizing* The members of a profession develop a structure. They create an association and try to set up a training programme. One starts colleague surveillance and attempts to get recognition (e.g. by the government and client organizations). There are two issues which receive particular attention. The first one is self-regulation. Members of the profession are convinced that they should decide about the

way in which professionals should do their work. It is at this stage that the profession will draft a code of conduct in order to regulate the behaviour of members.

A second issue is the recruiting of new members. For the continuity of the profession it is highly important that the profession recruits new members. This is the only way to uphold ideas and convictions. New members have to be socialized. They should identify with the goals and values of the profession. This is an important part of the professional training programme. So institutionalizing creates structures but also contributes to continuity.

The third stage is directed towards acquiring external support: *legitimizing*. The profession has to be recognized by others—principals, clients, the government, the general public. A profession has its own way to define problems and to handle them and it is important that such an approach be accepted by others. Only then will the profession gain credibility. The members are seen as experts and this stimulates the willingness to accept them as service providers.

It is possible that different professions are successful in getting different definitions accepted and so provide different services. Thus W&O psychologists have stated that successful performance is highly dependent on individual characteristics which can be measured with the aid of psychological tests. Many organizations, accepting this definition seek assistance from W&O psychologists when they hire new staff.

The lawyers point out different problems in the recruitment process. They define the situation as one whereby two parties try to reach agreement about obligations and compensation and offer their services for drafting contracts. Both types of expert have their own definition of the situation and are successful in selling their services to clients.

Professions are not static, they are subject to change. That has to do with problems and solutions. We live in a turbulent environment. Problems change and so too the profession, but also others come and develop new solutions. Therefore it can occur that a client, who has made use in the past of the services of a W&O psychologist for management selection, will decide now to make use of a consultant, who is not necessarily a W&O psychologist for executive search Constantly professionals are confronted with new demands and all kinds of competition.

2.3   The W&O psychologist today

It is questionable if the image of the W&O profession as it is today is still in accordance with the descriptions of the authors of the sixties. It would appear that, particularly due to exponential growth, a different situation has come into existence. In traditional literature the professional is seen as a service provider one who works for individual clients and does so his whole career. Examples are physicians and public notaries. The situation with W&O psychologists is, however, different. A large majority of W&O psychologists are not self-employed but are employed by organizations. And in such organizations many psychologists do not work with individuals, e.g. interviewing applicants but have other duties such as developing training programmes. The argument that the profession provides access to clients is nowadays not valid for many W&O psychologists. Instead of colleague surveillance one is subjected to supervision by the organization. The professional culture has lost its importance since such psychologists will orientate themselves more towards the organization by whom they are employed and less so towards the profession. A substantial number of similar psychologists will no longer become a member of the professional association.

This is even more the case since of late many new graduates take up positions which can also be filled by non-psychologists. Due to the enormous growth in the number of graduates, for most of them it is not possible to find employment in typical W&O positions, e.g. personnel selection. So they seek employment elsewhere in other positions. Nowadays there is a strong growth in new service positions for which there are no special training programmes available. Organizations hire university graduates and provide their own special training programmes.

So the traditional profession has undergone a change. There are many W&O psychology graduates but there is less interaction between W&O graduates. No longer is it one profession incorpo-

rating all graduates. This will be discussed at greater length later on.

3   THE DOMAIN

Thompson (1967) points out that each organization has to deal with two central questions: "What kind of products or services does one want to deliver?" "What kind of clients do you want to work for?" The way the organization tackles those questions is crucial to its survival. If one concentrates on products for which there is insufficient demand the organization will run into trouble. The same is true for clients. If the organization concentrates on clients who are not interested in the product or who cannot afford to buy it then it cannot be successful. The same goes for professions who have to cope with these same problems. A professional who offers his/her services, but discovers that clients are buying those services from his/her competitors has serious problems.

Professionals have to charge a fee. That can either be directly when the client is charged with a bill or indirectly by working for an organization and in receiving a salary. The client buys the services of a professional because he/she is convinced that the expertise of the professional is helpful in solving problems. The professional provides surplus value. The client pays the bill, in the expectation that the service will lead to an added value.

This distinguishes scientific work from professional work. With scientific work the central issue is truth. To what extent are statements truthful? Is a statement correct? In this context it is not important if the person who is making the statement is paid or not but with professional work this is different. The professional needs to make a living and the services he/she is providing have to have a surplus value for the client.

The choosing of a domain demands questioning if there are clients, who are willing to pay for services.

A researcher can be a professional so in that case he/she expects to be paid for doing research. In such cases he/she is confronted by the question if there is a client who is going to pay for her/his services, one for whom the researcher can deliver an added value.

A professional, who provides services, is confronted with scientific questions too. He/she has been trained as a scientist and cannot avoid coming up against all kinds of scientific questions when he/she is working for a client. A W&O psychologist involved in personnel selection has to deal with the validity and reliability questions about the instruments he/she is using. Maybe the client is not going to raise such questions but nevertheless his integrity will demand a critical attitude towards his own actions.

A domain is dynamic. The problems of clients change as does the knowledge and experience of professionals. Organizations operate in a turbulent environment and are constantly confronted by new demands. They ask professionals to assist them in meeting such new demands. And this may lead to all kinds of developments. It can also lead to adjusting existing approaches. Due to the enormous increase in knowledge and the increase in the number of professionals it is now possible to offer an extended range of services. The committee who in 1965 formulated guidelines for the American W&O training programme were well aware of this dynamic nature of the profession. It limited the guidelines for a period of five years and stipulated that by then the guidelines should be adjusted. (APA, 1965).

The past history of W&O psychology shows how the domain has been shaped by the continuous interaction with clients (see also Volume 1, Chapter 4). Practices in personnel selection have been very much shaped by events in the USA during the First and Second World Wars. Military leaders were confronted with acute problems of how to allocate conscripts to the many different positions in the modern military forces. To decide who were able to become an officer and who would be successful as a pilot. Psychologists had had some experience in allocating personnel, but were now presented with an enormous opportunity to try out their methods on a large scale.

This resulted in gigantic programmes like the Army Aviation Psychology Programme (1947). This programme was highly effective. It was not only accepted by the military forces but it also helped to have such approaches introduced into other organizations, e.g. in industry. Other clients became convinced that these approaches represented added values to their organization. Newly graduated psychologists started to offer such services to other clients. And so the developments in the military forces went to shape developments in the profession.

Similarly one can see developments in organizational psychology. An extensive programme "The American Soldier" dealt with all kinds of problems relating to morale, such as stress amongst bomber pilots flying over Germany, and that of soldiers on being repatriated, confronted with the problems of reintegration into society (Stouffer et al., 1949). Also here professionals were able to offer services which represented an added value to the client and again success opened the door to fresh clients. It helped to broaden the domain. Where formally it had been just industrial psychology, it had now became industrial/ organizational psychology.

These examples show how a profession can be influenced by events: clients with particular needs discover that professionals with a specific expertise can help them to solve problems. In such a way approaches can prove their worth, and will attract the attention of other clients. One may expect that also in the future such instances will go to shape the domain. Discussions on the domain are never closed. The domain has to be adjusted and will go on to be developed continuously. There is a continuous process of differentiation, institutionalizing and legitimization.

Domains are also threatened. Other professions also offer services and those may come to substitute those of the W&O psychologist. Thompson points out that a domain has to be defended. Personnel selection was, for a long time, a domain which belonged almost exclusively to psychologists. Now many others offer their services (e.g. outplacement consultancies, temping services, headhunters, personnel officers). This raises the question of how a domain should be defended: "Should psychologists react passively and hope that they will prevail or should they adopt a more active strategy?" This will be discussed later.

3.1 The domain of W&O psychology

In the past decades the domain of W&O psychology has become strongly differentiated. For a long time personnel selection was the core of the domain. In some European countries W&O psychology and selection were for the general public identical. Many individuals had at one time taken part in psychological test procedures and had become familiar with paper and pencil tests. Conscripts were required to complete psychological tests when drafted into the military forces. So testing was a familiar subject. The psychologists who worked as professionals in this field had much in common. The domain could be well defended. Psychologists could convince organizations that they had more expertise in the field than any other profession. Clients were convinced that the services had added volume. Others who tried to provide such services could be labelled as quacks (Thorndike 1949).

In the early period there were other services as well, e.g. research into safety measures, monotonous work, and leadership but this was less prominent than the work in personnel selection.

Particularly in the past twenty-five years the domain has been broadened and it seems that this differentiation process is set to continue. In this respect marked differences can be seen between countries. The differentiation process started early on in the US and somewhat later in Europe. In the Netherlands there has been a strong interest shown in organizational psychology while in France the interest has been minimal.

In 1965 the *American Psychologist* published guidelines for the training of W&O psychologists. These guidelines described the core of the domain. Three areas are pinpointed: personnel psychology, human factor psychology and industrial social psychology (the latter became organizational psychology in later years). To this core were added: industrial clinical psychology and marketing psychology (American Psychological Association, 1965).

In the same year Guion described the domain more or less similarly: engineering psychology, military psychology, consumer psychology, personnel psychology and industrial social psychology (Guion, 1965).

More recently ENOP, a network of European professors in W&O psychology has set up a reference model for W&O psychologists (Roe et al., 1994). This model also describes the core of the domain: personnel psychology, organizational psychology and work psychology. For each of these areas subjects are mentioned e.g. work psychology includes ergonomics, work and health, and stress management. ENOP points out that there are related specialties. These are areas where W&O psychologists are working but which apparently do not belong to the core. Examples are engineering psychology, traffic psychology, managerial psychology, consumer psychology and health psychology. These are areas where others are also active.

The differentiation process can lead to a breaking away of parts of the domain. An area may become more or less independent. Consumer psychology is an example. Guion includes it in his description of the domain but in the ENOP description it is a related specialty. Similarly engineering psychology appears to have become an independent area. Psychologists working in this area have started creating their own divisions in psychological associations.

The above description of the domain points out areas and sub-specializations. There are also descriptions on the content. De Wolff (1985) put together a directory of W&O psychologists working in European Universities, including the research topics of departments and individuals. There were 91 departments and 390 individuals included. The subjects most frequently mentioned were ergonomics, stress, work satisfaction, automation, functioning of groups, task design, training, selection, organizational structure and organizational development. All of these items were among those mentioned by at least 10% of the respondents.

Winterfeld (1992) performed a study in Germany on the work activities of W&O psychologists. Training was the most important activity (mentioned by 53% of his respondents), followed by selection (45%) organizational consulting (38%), personnel development (31%), clinical W&O psychology (18%) research and teaching (15%) and rehabilitation (12%). Other activities (like safety) did not reach the 10% threshold. A study among graduates from one Dutch university (de Greef, 1993) finds similar results: organizational development, training, organizational consulting, career guidance, clinical W&O psychology and selection. Striking is the strong increase in interest in training.

The *American Psychologist* of February 1990 describes "The changing face and place of work". It does not pretend to give a full description of the domain but three areas receive special attention: "Developing and maintaining competitiveness", "Developing leaders of tomorrow", and "Workplace wellbeing". It points out that organizations are continually confronted with new demands and that psychologists can help with finding the answers. Interesting in this approach is the description of the domain in terms of interaction between the client needs and the knowledge domain.

On looking through textbooks used for the training of W&O psychologists it strikes one that chapter titles used more than 60 years ago (Meyers, 1920, Viteles, 1930) are still pretty much the same as those used today. Viteles mentions individual differences, selection, job analysis, interviewing, safety training, industrial fatigue, motivation, maladjusted workers, problems of supervision and management. Also these days such subjects belong to the core of the domain.

From these descriptions one can see that there is continuity as well as development. There are subjects which receive attention over very long periods, like personnel selection. Other subjects have become more independent and valid for all subjects it is the fact that there is additional new knowledge and an adaptation to new demands.

Description of the domain may also serve the legitimizing process. They may mean to inform clients on what to expect from W&O psychologists.

Guion feels that W&O Psychology should concern itself with the relationship between humans and the world of work and more in particular with the adaptation of humans to the workplace and the people with whom they work and what they do to make a living. He mentions three subjects which he feels are essential: "identification of behavioural components and consequences of work performance", "identification

and utilization of talent and determination of the meaning of work".

The Netherlands Institute of Psychologists asked a committee to write a report on professional activities and the training of psychologists in the 21st century (Nederlands Instituut van Psychologen, 1991). In the report the authors state that the central issue is that humans have to adapt themselves to the everchanging environment. Particularly, technological developments have had a great impact on the task environment. Psychologists will have to assist people in this process of adaptation to new technology and in the creation of a technological environment on a human scale. Three types of interventions are proposed: "restructuring the environment", "improving a coping repertoire through learning new knowledge and skills", and "building up protection against stress".

W&O psychologists state all kind of goals. Goals commonly mentioned are improving effectiveness of behaviour and improving productivity. Another issue often mentioned is human dignity. Goals point out on what issues W&O psychologists should concentrate. These contribute to the dynamic nature of the domain.

The domain is broad. There are issues that may become a specialization in themselves, like ergonomics and consumer psychology. Because the domain is broad it is also more difficult to defend. One of the advantages of specialization and differentiation could be that the members of the new specialty will do more about the defending of their part of the domain.

3.2   Domain and growth

It has already been described how the domain develops but this did not fully take into account the rapid growth. The figures presented show the relative importance of subjects, but ten percent of W&O psychologists in 1960 is a very different number to ten percent in 1995. The number of service providers is increasing rapidly and will all these new providers find employment?

Striking is that the number of W&O psychologists that are taking up positions, which can also be filled by non-psychologists, is also increasing. Krijnen (1975) presented figures for the period (1963–1972) in the Netherlands. In that period the proportion of W&O psychologists holding a typical W&O position decreased from 62 to 56%. De Greef (1993) found only 15%, but these figures cannot be compared with those of Krijnen. Krijnen considered a national sample of W&O psychologists, and de Greef considered a sample of young graduates from one university. Nevertheless it appears that the number of W&O psychologists taking up non-psychologists' positions is on the increase. There are now numerous positions for which there is no specific university training programme available, but where employers feel that the W&O psychology training programme provides a good start (Rutte & de Wolff, 1994). W&O psychologists taking up such positions, do, often after some time, no longer identify with W&O psychology.

So it appears that there are three domains of W&O psychology which overlap, but that also have specific elements. The first domain is the one of the researchers. They usually work at universities. Besides doing research they also occupy themselves with teaching, either of W&O students or others. This domain is highly exclusive. To become a researcher at the university one has to be a qualified W&O psychologist. This domain is strongly defended. Applicants have to present a list of publications, preferably having appeared in international journals of high repute. Further researchers who want to publish articles have to have their manuscripts reviewed by peers. Colleague surveillance is very strong in this domain, not only regarding publications but also research grants. W&O psychologists working in these organizations strongly identify with the subject. The profession is an important frame of reference. Professionals see each other regularly at national and international conferences.

The second domain is different. Here it is the psychologists who provide services like selection and training. This is also a group which identifies with the profession. But their position is much weaker. There is competition from others. The domain is less exclusive. One wants to defend the domain but it is difficult to do this adequately. The domain is broad and it is difficult to define the borders.

The third domain is even broader. They are the people who have been trained as professional psychologists, but take up positions which can also be filled by other professionals. For such positions it is seen to be an advantage to have been trained as a psychologist, but there is no exclusiveness and the domain is hardly defensible. In 1976 Stanton pointed out in an APA book on career opportunities that there will be limited employment opportunities in traditional jobs. He foresaw opportunities in personnel administration and human resource development (Stanton, 1976). This also emerges from European studies.

Professionals working in this domain usually do not fit in with the traditional model. They do not occupy one position for a lifetime, such as physicians do, but pursue a career, which is a succession of positions. They are organization and career orientated.

It is possible to exclude this domain from W&O psychology but it make sense to include it for a number of reasons. Teaching W&O psychology is an important activity for the profession. At universities, teaching is usually tied to doing research. So even when graduates do not enter the second domain, it is attractive to train students in W&O psychology.

Furthermore the third domain has all kinds of relationships with the second domain. There is substantial overlap. Professionals in this area use W&O psychology knowledge and may even promote research.

4   WHO IS THE CLIENT?

Many psychologists will associate the word "client" with the code of conduct. Applicants taking part in a psychological test procedure are for psychologists the clients. However when Thompson discusses the client he means the person or the organization who pays for the services. So from this point of view it is the organization and not the applicant who is the client.

A professional psychologist has to seek clients who will pay for his/her services. In traditional professions the client issue is not so complicated. Professionals provide consulting hours in where clients can come to see them. The professional will send them a bill later. In W&O psychology only a small minority find themselves in this situation. The majority is employed by an organization from whom they receive a salary. In those circumstances they may deal with individuals (e.g. applicants) but it is the organization which pays for the services.

Thorndike (1949) added a chapter to his book on the personnel selection programme and the public (p.312). He nicely puts into words the need to find a client.

> A basic fact that every personnel psychologist needs to appreciate, whether he is working in industry, in civil service, or in the armed forces, is that the broad administrative decisions which determine the conditions under which he is to work and even the question of whether he is to continue to work will be made not by him but by the administrative superiors. Some person or persons in the top levels of management will have the power to decide that there is to be a personnel selection programme and that psychological tests are to be used. Someone will obtain funds for the programme. Someone will decide how much time of job applicants is to be made available for testing, and how much testing can be done with employees already on the job. The psychologist may be consulted on all these points. He will certainly have a opportunity to express his opinions and offer his recommendations. But the general decisions on the matters of policy will not be his.

> This dependence on others for the continuing support of his activities raises a new set of practical problems which the personnel psychologist must face. They are problems of salesmanship. A personnel programme necessarily includes a selling programme, to guarantee continuing acceptance of and support for the programme. It is of critical importance to sell the programme to those members of top man-

agement who have powers of life or death over the programme.

It is not always the top management who makes the decisions. There are organizations where also others have influence on the decision making. An example can be found in universities, where programmes are discussed in councils, and where the university is often dependent upon government support. So there are several parties having an influence on the life and death of programmes.

Selling is not an entirely rational process. Codes of conduct have some rules obliging the psychologist to give a fair representation of his/her services and qualifications. But the client is free, and can basically decide about "life or death" of a programme. And the client does not always use rational arguments. To clients a very important consideration is if the psychologist feels in the first instance an interest in his needs. There may be concern that the professional is more involved in his own interests (income, advancement or prestige among colleagues). Clients often expect to see signs that the professional is loyal to the client or a client organization. So the relationship is certainly not a neutral one. Usually the professionals have to prove themselves to the client and persuade him that the services have added value.

Psychologists often want to use arguments showing that these activities contribute to the profit of the organization. For example by using psychological tests the organization can hire more qualified applicants and these will contribute towards higher effectiveness and higher profit. Psychologists employed by an organization often strongly identify with the interests of that organization; particularly those who have to sell the programmes do so. Organizations expect their managers and experts to look after the interests of the organization. New members of that group when they enter the organization are taught in the socialization process similarly to do so.

At the end of the sixties, in the period of student revolts, this created tension. There were heated discussions about the position of workers and a rather hostile climate developed against employers. Political parties were for the introduction of a form of participation and industrial democracy. Psychologists working for industrial organizations were often seen as "lackeys of management". Discussions developed as to whether such psychologists, as well as personnel officers, should not in the first place identify with the interests of the workers. Such discussions took off first in the universities and schools for professional training. This created quite some role conflict and role ambiguity (Van Bastelaer & Van Beers, 1982). In that period there were groups of psychologists working at universities (e.g. the Themagroep Noord at the University of Groningen) who expressed their loyalty towards workers. They wanted to assist workers in their struggles with employers. This approach was not appreciated by most of their colleagues but did attract interest on the part of students.

There were also psychologists who felt it might be better to work for the labour unions but who soon discovered that there were very few positions available in such organizations.

Yet other psychologists, working for universities, chose to concentrate on issues which raised fewer discussions. Interest in personal selection declined rapidly; new issues such as industrial democracy and participation attracted much attention. Where formerly the field was known as industrial psychology, the name "Work and Organizational Psychology" came into use. This was in line with the broadening of the domain and the substantial number of W&O psychologists taking up positions in non-industrial organizations.

The changing political climate, the discussions in the universities and the changes in the profession certainly had an impact on the position of psychologists in industrial organizations.

While formerly they had identified with the management, they now dealt with complex situations. Role senders in the professional associations and in the universities expressed different expectations to those of management and workers councils. Decision-making processes about programmes of psychologists were more complex too. This episode in the development of W&O psychology shows that the relationship with the client is influenced by ideological and political issues and that strong emotions might be involved. It is clearly more complex than as described by Thorndike in 1949. Selling a programme is not an entirely rational activity. In organizations there are always conflicting interests and service providers can be caught out because parties try to use the services of the service provider for their own interests. This is why law and codes of conduct are important, because through such laws a better balanced decision can be made, to recognize the different interests involved.

5 MANAGING THE PROFESSION

"Defending the domain" and "choosing a client" suggests that within a profession choices are made and that there should be the presence of some kind of managerial system. How then is a profession managed?

To start with there is a professional association with a board and various divisions.

Board members can stimulate discussion, approve programmes, approach government organizations, etc., but that is not all. Universities train new professionals. There may be general outlines for training programmes, but it is in the way universities set up their programmes that they contribute to the shaping of the domain.

Within the profession there is a continuous discussion on all kind of topics, evident from the president's yearly addresses, and articles written by members. In journals like the *American Psychologist* one can find such articles, and follow the ongoing discussion as to what course of action the profession should be taking.

Mok (1973) points out that in all professions there are factions defending certain views. There are always views that will compete with one another. Competition can be on scientific issues: which theory explains the existing data better. But more often the discussion is on values: such an approach represents a higher added value to clients. These factions give it their own interpretations.

A classical conflict is the one about priorities. Some defend the idea that the profession should concentrate on enlarging the knowledge base before concentrating on serving clients. Others feel that the profession should concentrate on a client's needs and learn in the process. This is the kind of conflict which comes up in almost all professions.

In The Netherlands it was Duijker (1977, 1978) who strongly defended the idea that psychologists should enlarge the knowledge base. He constantly stressed that the knowledge base was too small and therefore, hardly an opportunity was given for professional psychologists to serve clients. Others pointed out that psychological knowledge is highly valued in finding answers to problems within organizations and see clearly a place for professional psychologists in providing services to clients. Within a profession there are conflicting views all the time. In discussions one tries to convince others. Researchers stress that more resources should be allocated to research projects and feel that basic issues should be included more in training programmes. Service providers want more support from the professional association in order to improve their position towards clients and competing professionals. They want to have training programmes placing more attention on practical problems.

Mok points out that within each profession there is usually a dominant faction—a group of professionals who have been successful in making their own views prevail. Their definition of the situation is accepted by the majority of professionals. Members of that faction are elected to key positions. They are members of the board of the association but can also be appointed as professors in teaching and research programmes. In such positions they defend the views of the dominant faction. Their views are accepted because the majority of those in the profession are of the opinion that this offers the best approach to satisfying the demands the profession has to meet. The views of the dominant faction are usually also more acceptable to parties outside the profession, such as the clients and the government.

A dominant faction is not necessarily homogeneous. It can be a coalition of different interests. Schönpflug (1993) cites an example from the beginning of the twentieth century. Psychologists needed to establish themselves in the universities, but met opposition from the philosophers who often occupied the chairs in psychology. A coalition was formed from experimental and applied psychologists. What brought them together was the mutual need to get established within the university. Schönpflug has doubts about the wisdom of this coalition.

Dominant coalitions are not always successful at staying in power. Due to internal and external changes the views of the dominant coalition can prove less adequate and show a lower survival value. Other factions may be able to take over the position, as happened in the late fifties and early sixties in some European countries.

The first generation of psychologists in The Netherlands was very much client-orientated. Heymans, the founder of Dutch psychology, expected "that psychology would contribute to reason and happiness. People seek to come to peace with the world and themselves and psychology tries to provide the knowledge to do so. It will however take a long time before psychology can do so. But it certainly will" (see Eisinga, 1978). Dutch psychology was very much influenced by German psychology. The approach was directed at "understanding" and not on "prediction". Holistic methods (such as projective techniques) were used.

After the Second World War, younger psychologists discovered how much progress had been made in the USA, particularly in the period between 1935–1955. A new generation of psychologists started eagerly to read American literature. Van Strien (1988) shows in a study how psychologists who became professors before 1960 mainly quoted German literature in their thesis. Those who became professors after 1960 quoted Anglo-Saxon literature (usually over 80% of their references).

The first generation of psychologists disappeared mainly during the fifties and early sixties. With a new generation came a new dominant faction. This new faction was not client-orientated, but wanted in the first case to enlarge the knowledge base. "More research is needed".

The change is understandable. The first generation had been highly successful in making psychology acceptable to the general public and selling the subject to clients. This group of psychologists was small in the Netherlands; before 1940 there were only 50. It is interesting to see what positions some acquired in the Dutch society. One became a prime minister, another became a cabinet minister. A third one was a member of several boards of large companies, a fourth was a counsellor to the Queen, and in addition there were a number of professors. Their influence in society was considerable.

But the knowledge base of the discipline was not strong, and when a new generation advocated concentrating on enlarging that knowledge base, they easily prevailed. New appointments in universities were mainly psychologists who had demonstrated that they could do research.

In a changing environment the dominant faction can change once again. In the USA the number of practising psychologists, particularly clinical psychologists, has increased considerably, and one can see that, starting in the late seventies, all kind of struggles take place in the psychological association. Clinical psychologists and university psychologists have their own candidates for the president of the association. The APA has tried hard to set up programmes for both groups. Nevertheless the scientifically orientated psychologists have established a new association (APS).

Processes within a professional association are of a political nature. There are views and interests which are defended by individuals and groups but the processes help the profession to accommodate new demands. Also professions operate in a turbulent environment. Clients, but also the government, place new demands and the profession has to find ways of answering them. Through the discussions and struggles, answers are formed.

6   THE TRAINING OF THE WORK AND ORGANIZATIONAL PSYCHOLOGIST

When we discussed how professions came into being it was pointed out how important training programmes are. For the continuity of the profession one has to recruit members, and such new members have to be trained. They have to become familiar with the approaches and values of the profession. A training programme is not only a transfer of knowledge, it is also a socializing process. Trainers are also role models. They familiarize new members with the expectations had by colleagues, clients and other role senders. And in particular they familiarize the new members with how the profession defines problems and how problems are approached. New members learn about the domain, and how clients can be best served.

Such training does not only take place in lecture rooms. There has to be a period where new members go out and work under the supervision of experienced professionals. Gradually new members become more autonomous and become full members, fulfilling their own roles. Training is highly important to the profession. It not only offers continuity but it also safeguards the professional culture.

Just as there is continuous debate in the profession on how problems should be defined and approached, there is also continuous discussion on training. Also here there are competing factions and a dominant faction.

Professional associations usually have quite some influence on training programmes both formally and informally. It is often members of the dominant faction who hold key positions both in the university, as in the association. Presidents of the association are often professors. Many members of important committees in the association are employed by universities. Officers in the association are often involved in accreditation and evaluation of training programmes.

To W&O psychologists a training programme is in the first instance training in psychology. W&O psychology is a field of application and a specialization. In The Netherlands Duijker (1959) developed a model for the psychology training programme which was widely adopted, and even today is recognized. According to this model training should start with basic subjects like social psychology and experimental psychology, followed by introduction into fields of application like clinical psychology and W&O psychology. After this one specializes either in a basic subject or in a certain field of application.

This model proved acceptable to a wide group of professionals. So there is clearly a broad coalition supporting this model, yet nevertheless Duijker's model has never been fully implemented. There have always been groups who wanted it to be modified in some way. But the overall approach remains a highly appreciated one, and has been mentioned in discussions over the decades.

Psychologists are also involved in training programmes of other professionals, e.g. pedagogues, business administrators, economists, physicians. Graduates of such programmes often compete in the labour market with W&O psychologists. Psychologists have even initiated new training programmes (e.g. agoges, personnel managers). Nevertheless the W&O psychology programme continues to recruit large numbers of students and has been fairly stable over the past decades. However, the competition in the labour market urges educators to make up their mind about what they want to accomplish. If those who graduate do not find adequate employment this will provoke all kind of tensions and might lead eventually to outside intervention. As a result the willingness to support such programmes might become eroded.

ENOP, a network of European W&O professors, has set up a reference model for W&O training programmes (Roe et al., 1994). This model corresponds with Duijker's approach; it also starts with basic subjects and introductions, after which the specialization in W&O psychology follows. It distinguishes three streams: personnel psychology, organizational psychology, and work psychology. For each stream courses are specified and described including the literature which can be used for such courses. Before setting up this reference model a review was made of European training programmes, thus it is based on a better definition of the domain of W&O psychology. The model is a good base for accreditation of training programmes

Also the ENOP reference model clearly elect for a psychology training programme. Students should first of all become familiar with psychology. Employers often state that they look for applicants who have been seen to have mastered a certain subject but who are also familiar with the setting wherein the knowledge can be applied (Rutte & de Wolff, 1994; de Wolff & Hurley, 1994). In university training programmes both aspects can be seen. The ENOP model gives priority to the subject of psychology.

This is also clear from a study done by de Wolff

& Shimmin (1994). They held a survey among 24 European W&O professors. Their respondents were clearly attached to a psychological training programme. When, due to economizing measures, programmes had to be reduced one tried to retain the psychology section, and reduce the orientation in other subjects and in the work setting. The general idea was that such orientation should take place after the completion of the university programme. Such an approach is contrary to the one followed in business administration programmes. There the emphasis is much more on orientation, instead of mastering a particular discipline. It appears that employers appreciate the psychologists's approach (Rutte & de Wolff, 1994)

7 THE PROFESSIONAL ASSOCIATION

The position of the professional association has changed due to a number of developments.

A first development has to do with psychology having become an established discipline. For W&O psychology, the establishment process (as described in section 2 of this chapter) was more or less completed during the sixties. For example it was in this period most Dutch universities established chairs in W&O psychology. Psychology, including W&O psychology had become a recognized discipline. So the focus changed from that of becoming recognized to other issues, having more to do with expansion. Such a new stage brings its own problems. Objectives are no longer so common and inspiring to all the members of the profession. Factions within the profession are more inclined to pursue their own interests. Associations and activities are highly dependent upon volunteers. Members spend a lot of time on administrative activities and committee work. To employ staff is costly and increases the membership fee. This in turn might discourage professionals from becoming a member, or may lead to the discontinuation of membership. Several authors point out that professionals are dedicated people (Hall, 1969; Kast & Rosenzweig, 1970). But when the goals of the association become less inspiring the willingness to take part in such activities will decrease.

There has been a clear shift seen in membership. For a long time university psychologists were in the majority but during the past two decades the number of practising psychologists, particularly clinical and health psychologists has increased enormously. Goodstein (1988) reports that in the USA between 1976 and 1985 the percentage of psychologists working at universities decreased from 47 to 34. In the same period the number of psychologists working in health care increased from 37 to 46.5. Pion et al. (1996) present figures about psychology PhDs. In 1973 about 56% of the psychologists who were working full time were employed by colleges and universities. In 1991 their share had dropped to 38%. Howard et al. (1986) presents a table showing that in 1972 the number of Health Service Provider PhDs surpassed the number of Academic/Research Subfield PhDs. Since then the former has continued to grow rapidly while the latter has declined. So there is on the one hand a change in the composition of the profession, but also on the other a clear shift in the kind of employment.

In Europe the decrease has been even larger. Employment opportunities at universities are bleak; graduates have to look for employment elsewhere (de Wolff & Shimmin, 1994)

The shift has had consequences for the associations. University staff, having a dominant position in APA, were confronted by clinical and health psychologists wanting to take over the dominant position. APA has as its objective the promotion of psychology as a science, as well as a profession. APA has made a great effort to support both the researchers, who want to advance psychology and to increase the knowledge base and to advance psychologists as health providers. Nevertheless a group of university psychologists have established a new association: The American Psychological Society. This did not however have an effect on the membership of APA, there was uninterrupted growth (see Koocher, 1996).

The struggle between academic psychologists and health providers puts the W&O psychologists in a special position. They now go more their own way. In the USA the *Society for Industrial and Organizational Psychology* has become an independent organization. In Europe the *European Association of Work and Organizational Psychologists* was founded in1981. This association has relationships with national divisions, but also has allowed individual membership. This organization concentrates on organizing conferences and promoting the exchange of information.

There is a substantial difference between the association in the USA and European associations. The APA is, in comparison with European associations, a very big one. It has a staff of over 500 (Fowler, 1996) and a budget of about 60 million dollars. European associations have a much more modest size. For example, in 1996 the Dutch Association, NIP had a staff of 25 and a budget of 3.6 million guilders (approx. 1.8 million dollars). There is a federation of European associations, EFPPA but this federation does not have its own professional office. Associations mainly operate on a national level. The APA having more critical mass can operate on a more professional level. One activity which receives much attention is the influencing of government decision making processes (Goodstein, 1988). Government is by far the most important financier of research programmes, directly or indirectly and is also a very important employer and in so doing, has enormous impact on the development of psychology. The APA monitors government programmes and makes sure that government officials and politicians are made aware of what psychologists can contribute. When there are hearings in Congress the APA presents the psychologist's view. This can be seen as part of the legitimizing process as described in section 2 of this chapter. A profession has its own definition of problems and attempts to make others to accept these definitions. By presenting carefully documented views to the government APA is defending the domain of psychologists.

APA has been doing this for several years. In the beginning this was done by a separate organization because some members were sceptical about lobbying. Now it is a regular activity and the viewpoints presented at hearings are regularly published in the *American Psychologist* and in the *Psychological Monitor*. An advantage of this openness is that psychologists are more accountable for their views. Other professions can endorse but also dispute them. It stimulates debate. This is not only important for the profession but also for clients.

In Europe this type of debate is much more restricted; this is probably due to the smaller size of the associations.

Another effort has been made by the American Psychological Society. This society set up a committee, chaired by Milton Hakel, which identified six areas of broad national concern: Productivity in the workplace, schooling and literacy, the ageing society, drug and alcohol abuse, health and violence in America. The committee invited societies to prepare specific research initiatives that would be presented to Congress and federal and other agencies. It wanted to define tangible problems in the real world, describe current knowledge and to identify key issues that needed to be investigated (American Psychological Society, 1992). Also this is an example of where psychologists get involved in discussions on social problems and where they try to contribute to the solution of such problems.

Other tasks for associations are the accreditation of training programmes and licensing. Where there is substantial economizing, training programmes are threatened. It is important that quality is monitored, to make sure that the graduates meet standards set for good practice and research.

that others claim that they are more qualified, or one can feel more qualified oneself.

In the course of time there have been marked shifts. Until the sixties it seemed that sociologists would acquire a very strong position. At that time sociology was popular with students but later on the interest decreased. In The Netherlands, during the seventies andragogy, a study usually located in the pedagogy departments was highly popular. But partly due to the intervention of the Ministry of Education during the eighties this programme has almost disappeared. Nowadays business administration graduates (MBA) comprise the most important competitors (de Wolff & Shimmin, 1994). (This is not the case for East Europe, where such programmes do not yet exist.) Business administration was enormously popular during the eighties and early nineties, while numbers are decreasing in the second half of the nineties, yet the study remains still quite popular.

Competition also exists in other areas. For example selection services nowadays are provided by head-hunters and mediators who often offer packages of selection and recruitment. Those who offer such services are often non-psychologists.

These developments show that positions can change considerably. Professions despite having a strong position can lose this in the course of time and newcomers can capture a substantial part of the market.

8 RELATIONSHIP WITH OTHER DISCIPLINES

Other professionals offer services or apply for positions and compete with W&O psychologists. The domain is not exclusive. Sometimes psychologists cooperate with other professionals, e.g. psychologists and sociologists working together as organizational consultants. But there is also direct competition, e.g. when different professionals apply for the same position. The relationship with other disciplines is ambivalent. Sometimes one feels that through cooperation one can offer better services. One will also experience

9 THE RELATIONSHIP WITH THE GOVERNMENT

The government has much influence on the profession. This is partly because the government is a big employer and also, through funding, indirectly has much influence on employment but also regulates society through laws and programmes. When the government drafts laws and sets up programmes it has its own definition of problems. Such definitions can be in agreement with the views of psychologists but can also be very different. Governments strive to stimulate employment, to prevent discrimination and to improve health. They are constantly busy developing programmes. How such programmes are shaped is very much dependent on the perception it has on causes. If one feels that health problems are caused by stress, one looks for another means to solve the problem than when one feels problems are created by inadequate food or poor sanitation. In western democracies there is a continuous debate about what government should do to improve a situation. There are always competing views and parties who try to influence the government.

For the profession there are two kind of problems. One is government can develop programmes which interfere with the services provided by the profession. The other kind of problem has to do with knowledge which is available and is relevant for the government programmes. Should the profession take action to bring the knowledge to the attention of the government?

There are a number of examples where government programmes interfered with services provided by W&O psychologists. In the fifties and sixties W&O psychologists constructed biographical inventories for personnel selection. They tried to find items which discriminate between applicants performing well and those performing poorly. Their interest in the actual contents of the items was very limited. The real interest was in prediction. But the applicants had gained a different impression, and complained about the contents of the items. They felt that psychologists had not respected their privacy by asking questions about issues which were none of their business. Eventually the Congress organized hearings (see the *American Psychologist*, 1965, no. 11). It is still interesting to read about the discussions which developed, and to see how psychologists were forced to rethink the issue and to change their mind. The government intervention started a discussion in the profession and psychologists had to redefine their definition of the problem. Similarly, the government's interventions to prevent discrimination forced psychologists to rethink their selection approaches. Government interventions can force professions to review their definitions of problems. It is striking that psychologists appeared often surprised by such interventions. They thought they

were dealing with a psychological and scientific issue and were insufficiently aware of the political nature of such issues. It is also likely that in the future there will be interventions. Since the domain has become so broad the chances of confrontations appear to be greater.

The other issue has to do with the relevant knowledge. Setting up programmes is usually preceded by discussions in parliament and in the press. This is a period in which individuals and interest groups present their views and try to influence the decision-making processes. It is also a period in which governments consult experts and councils. It is during these interaction processes that programmes are shaped and where governments seek support for the programmes in order to minimize conflicts.

Psychological research turns up new knowledge which often might be very useful for setting up programmes. Often such knowledge is brought to the attention of the government through councils and experts. There are issues however where, either through insufficient research or inadequate use of existing knowledge, programmes prove inadequate. This poses the question whether psychologists should perhaps present their own views in the discussions. Recently the president of the largest labour union in The Netherlands complained that social scientists did too little to study important issues and make their voice heard. In the 1996 meeting of the Dutch association a vice-chairman of a political party, a W&O psychologist by training, also complained that W&O psychologists did not make themselves heard enough.

The APA has chosen an approach whereby views are regularly presented, and so doing become part of the discussion. The APA also monitors government programmes in order to prevent confrontations, which happened in the cases of privacy and discrimination. The government is an important role sender for W&O psychologists. The professional association can do much to structure the interaction between the profession and government but for this one needs a strong association. When many W&O psychologists orientate themselves towards the organization they work for, instead of the profession, this may lead to withering away of those activities.

10 THE FUTURE OF THE WORK AND ORGANIZATIONAL PSYCHOLOGY PROFESSION

How is the W&O profession likely to develop? In 1981 de Wolff, Shimmin and de Montmollin published a number of scenarios:

- *Laissez-faire*, representing a situation of free for all in which market forces, government policies and environmental factors shape the development.
- *Reform from within*, whereby the profession itself wants to shape the developments.
- *Multidisciplinary approaches*, linked to the question of reform, but whereby W&O psychology is seen as developing within a multidisciplinary context.
- *Giving psychology away*, psychologists will concentrate on passing on knowledge to all who use it in the interest of human welfare (Miller, 1960).
- *Retreat*, to traditional protected areas of industrial psychology, less readily accessible to non-psychologists.
- *Withering away*, a pessimistic scenario, referring to the possibility of work psychology gradually ceasing to exist in its own right as a result of appearing no longer relevant to those on whom it is dependent (e.g. students, clients).
- *Opting out*, individual psychologists cease to identify with the discipline and describe themselves by functional occupational titles.

Ten years on de Wolff and Shimmin (1994) asked some European colleagues to indicate how they thought the discipline had developed during the eighties and what they expected would happen during the nineties. There was a striking difference in the appreciation of the two periods. For the eighties the *laissez-faire* scenario was seen as being the best description. But for the nineties one foresaw the "reform from within" and the "multidisciplinary" scenario. Apparently the respondents expected a less passive approach and a greater need to shape the profession. Pessimistic

scenarios like "retreat" and "withering away" were not supported by these respondents. The situation at the beginning of the eighties was clearly different from the one at the beginning of the nineties. During the seventies "withering" away had appeared to be a realistic scenario due to the lack of interest on the part of students for this study. During the seventies however the subject became popular again, and the profession was growing rapidly. It is understandable that the W&O professors did not support the "retreat" and "withering away" scenarios.

For the next decade three developments appear to shape the profession. The first one has to do with universities. Universities are mainly financed by the government, but governments struggle with deficits, and try to reduce costs. This has already gone on for a long period, but is particularly pertinent for the eighties and the nineties. Governments in Europe, wanting to meet the criteria for the monetary union are obliged to reduce their deficits. This means there is pressure on reducing staff and reducing the amount of time available for training programmes. On the other hand there is a strong feeling that countries who spend much on research and a well-educated workforce will perform better. So there is also a tendency to allocate more resources to excellent researchers. In order to find excellent researchers one has to look for publications, preferably printed in journals with a high quotation index. The result is that these days there is now more competition for more scarce resources. It means that university staff focus much more on publishing and spend less time on other activities (de Wolff & Roe, 1994). It may go to enlarge the gap between research and work in practice.

A second development is within organizations. There is more global competition and companies used to holding strong positions suddenly experiencing crisis situations. There is need for flexibility, commitment, increased productivity, more teamwork, more customer orientation and many other changes. There is less security had by employees, seeking different careers. To what extent will W&O psychologists help to meet such new demands? Clients seek help; what consequences will this have for the profession?

A third development has to do with the labour

market. The enormous increase in students is leading to a situation where graduates will find insufficient employment in traditional positions. More graduates will have to take positions which are not specifically meant for psychologists but can also be filled by other professionals. When they take up such positions, the relationship with the profession weakens; a substantial number of graduates will cease to identify with W&O psychology. Consequently they do not become a member of the professional association.

These are three very different developments, each placing their own demands on the profession. To be successful in publishing one may specialize but to be a consultant for an organization, trying to meet new demands one needs a broad orientation. Such wide demands are difficult to meet. It might lead to the university and the practitioners growing even wider apart.

In a *laissez-faire* scenario each of these three developments will take its own course. Scientists will look for interesting research questions and their position within the universities. Practitioners will concentrate on providing services to clients, and those who cease to identify with psychology will pursue other interests.

In the "reform" scenario the focus has to be the cooperation between these three groups. New developments in society require all kinds of research and the developing of new approaches to problems. The knowledge base of psychology has to be enlarged but the willingness to pay for this will be dependent on the perceived value for society. Although it often appears that the scientists and practitioners are not aware of the importance of cooperation, they have to be partners. Reform means very much a dominant faction which concentrates on the strengthening of unity in psychology.

REFERENCES

Abelson, R.P. (1981). Psychological status of the script concept. *American Psychologist, 36*, 715–729.

American Psychological Association. Division of Industrial Psychology (Committee on Education Policy) (1959). Professional education in industrial psychology: A statement of policy. *American Psychologist, 14*, 233–234.

American Psychological Association. Division of Industrial Psychology (1965). Guidelines for doctoral education in industrial psychology. *American Psychologist, 20*, 822–831.

American Psychological Society: Human capital initiative. *Observer, Special Issue*, February, 1992.

Army Air Force Aviation Psychology Research Programme Reports. (1947). Washington: Government Printing Office.

Bastelaer, A. van, & Beers, W. van (1982). *Organisatiestress en de personeelsfunctionaris*, Lisse.

Diaz, R., & Quintanilla I. (1992). La identidad professional del psicologo en el Estado Espanol. *Papeles del Psicologo, 52*, 22–74.

Drunen P. van, & Breyer, M. (1994). Meer en meer, als maar meer. *De Psycholoog, 29*(1), 16–21.

Duijker, H.C.J. (1959). Nomenclatuur en systematiek der psychologie. *Nederlands Tijdschrift voor de Psychologie, XIV*, 176–217.

Duijker, H.C.J. (1977). De psychologie en haar toekomst. Wat gebeurt er met de psychologie? De verantwoordelijkheid van de psycholoog. *De Psycholoog, XII*(2), 253–358, 415–422, 556–562.

Duijker, H.C.J. (1978). Dramatisering vs nuchterheid. Bij wijze van dagsluiting. NIP jubileumprijsvraag. *De Psycholoog, XIII*(1), 309, 256–266, 561–565.

Eisinga, L.K.A. (1978) *Geschiedenis van de Nederlandse Psychologie.* Deventer: Van Loghum Slaterus.

Fowler, R.D. (1996). Report of the Chief Executive Officer. *American Psychologist, 46*(7), 667–674.

Goodstein, L.D. (1988). The growth of the American Association. *American Psychologist, 43*(7), 491–498.

Greef, T. de (1993). *Beroepsuitoefening van arbeid-en organisatiepsychologen (2). Verslag onderzoeksproject naar de beroepsuitoefening van A&O– psychologen die in Nijmegen afgestudeerd zijn tussen 1984 en 1992.* Scriptie. Katholieke Universiteit Nijmegen.

Groot, A.D. de (1971). *Een minimale methodologie op sociaal wetenschappelijke basis.* Rede uitgesproken bij de aanvaarding van het hoogleraarsambt. Den Haag: Mouton.

Guion, R.M. (1965). Industrial psychology as an academic discipline. *American Psychologist, 20*, 815–821.

Hall, R.H. (1969). *Occupation and social structure.* Englewood Cliffs, NJ: Prentice-Hall.

Holtzer, F.H.J.M. (1984). Is er toekomst voor psychologen? *De Psycholoog, XIX*(6), 257–266.

Howard, A. et al. (1986). The changing face of American Psychology. *American Psychologist, 41*(12), 1311–1327.

Kast, F.E., & Rosenzweig, J.E. (1970). *Organization and management: A systems approach.* New York: McGraw-Hill.

Katz, D. & Kahn, R.L. (1978). *The social psychology of organizations* (2nd ed.) New York: Wiley.

Koocher, G.P. (1996). Report of the Treasurer. *American Psychologist*, *51*(8), 797–804.

Krijnen, G. (1975). *Ontwikkeling functievervulling van psychologen. Deel I.* Nijmegen: Instituut voor toegepaste sociologie.

Krijnen, G. (1976). *Ontwikkeling functievervulling van psychologen. Deel II.* Nijmegen: Instituut voor toegepaste sociologie.

Meyers, C.S. (1920). *Mind and work.* London: University of London Press.

Miller, L.A. (1960). Psychology as a mean of promoting human welfare. *American Psychologist*, *24*(12), 1063–1075.

Ministerie van Onderwijs en Wetenschappen (1995). Hoger Onderwijs in Cijfers.

Mok, L.A. (1973). *Beroepen in actie. bijdrage tot beroepensociologie.* Meppel: Boom.

Nederlands Instituut van Psychologen (1991). *Psychologie en Psycholoog in de 21 e eeuw. Preadvies over professionele werkuitvoering en opleiding.* Amsterdam.

Nijsten, J. (1984). *Beroepsuitoefening van arbeids-en organisatiepsychologen.* Scriptie. Katholieke Universiteit Nijmegen.

Pion, G.M. et al. (1996). The shifting gender composition of psychology. Trends and implication for the discipline. *American Psychologist*, *51*(5), 509–528.

Peiro, J.M., & Munduate, L. (1994). Work and organisational psychology in Spain. *Applied Psychology: An International Review*, *43*(2) 231–274.

Prieto, J.M. (1991). *The study of psychology in Spain.* Paper. Complutense University Madrid.

Quintanilla, I., & Diaz, R. (1992). *Some domeographic and economical characteristics of professional psychologists.* Paper. University of Valencia.

Roe, R.A. Coetsier, P., Levy Leboyer, C.L., Peiro, C.M., & Wilpert, B. (1994). The teaching of work and organizational psychology in Europe: Toward a development of a reference model. *The European Work and Organizational Psychologist*, *4*(4), 355–365.

Rosenzweig, M.R. (1992). Psychological science around the world. *American Psychologist*, *47*(6), 718–722.

Rutte, C.G., & Wolff, Ch.J. de (1994). Naar een nieuw profiel van de opleiding tot A&O psycholoog. *De Psycholoog*, *29*(2), 61–64.

Sardin, T.R., & Allen, V.L. (1968–1969). Role theory. In G. Lindzey & E. Aronson (Eds), *The Handbook of Social Psychology:* New York: Random House.

Schönpflug, W. (1993). Applied Psychology: Newcommer with a long tradition. *Applied Psychology: An International Review*, *42*(1), 5–30.

Stanton, E.S. (1976). Alternative career directions for the industrial organizational psychologist. In P.J. Woods (Ed.), *Career Opportunities for Psychologists.* American Psychological Association.

Stouffer, S.A., Suchman, E.A., DeVinney, L.C., Star, S.A., & Williams, R.M. (1949). *The American Soldier.* New York: John Wiley and Sons.

Strien, P.J. van (1978a). *Om de kwaliteit van het bestaan. Contouren van een emanciperende psychologie.* Meppel: Boom.

Strien, P.J. van (1978b). Vermaatschappelijking van de psychologie. Psychologen in de voorhoede. *De psycholoog, XII*(1), 211–219, 365–369.

Strien, P.J. van (1988). De Nederlandse psychologie in het internationale krachtenveld. *De Psycholoog*, *23*(10), 575–585.

Thompson, J.D. (1967). *Organizations in action.* New York: McGraw-Hill.

Thorndike, R. L. (1949). *Personnel selection. Test and measurement techniques.* New York: John Wiley & Sons.

Urbina-Soria, J., & Giron-Hidalgo, B (1992). *Past, present and perspectives of the largest psychology training in the world: The school of psychology, national university of Mexico.* Paper presented at the 25th International Congress of Psychology, Brussels, July, 1992.

Viteles, M.S. (1930). *Industrial Psychology.* New York: Norton.

Wegman, C. (1985). *Psycho-analysis and cognitive psychology. A formalization of Freud's earlier theory.* London: London Academic Press.

Winterfeld, U. (1992). *Industrial and organizational psychology in the Federal Republic of Germany.* Paper presented at the European Congress of W&O/ Psychology at Alicante, April, 1992.

Wolff, Ch.J. de (1985). *Directory of work and organizational psychology.* Report University of Nijmegen.

Wolff, Ch.J. de, & Hurley, J. (1994). The changing nature of the profession. Overview of panel discussions in six European countries. *The European work and Organizational Psychologist.* *4*(4), 343–353.

Wolff, Ch.J. de, & Roe R.A. (1994). Onderzoeksbeoordeling beoordeeld. *U&H, Tijdschrift voor wetenschappelijk onderwijs*, *40*(5).

Wolff, Ch.J. de, & Shimmin, S. (1994). Complexities and choices: Work psychology in Europe. *The European Work and Organizational Psychologist*, *4* (4), 333–341.

Wolff, Ch.J. de, Shimmin, S., & de Montmollin, M. (1981). *Conflicts and Contradictions.* London: Academic Press.

Wolfle, D. (1947). Annual Report of the Executive Secretary. *American Psychologist*, *2*, 516–520.

4

History of the Psychology of Work and Organization

Sylvia Shimmin and Pieter J. van Strien

INTRODUCTION

Why include a chapter on history in a handbook intended to give an overview of the current "state of the art" in the psychology of work and organization? Many would argue that all that is valuable from the past persists in present theory and practice, the residue being of little interest or relevance to contemporary students of what is a "down to earth" field of psychology, except perhaps for its curiosity value.

We maintain that, on the contrary, there is much to be learned from history. In the first place, knowledge of past failures and successes—knowledge that is partially lost—can help us in our present search for solutions. There is substance in the saying that those who ignore the past are condemned to repeat its mistakes. Second, the basic approach followed by psychologists over the years does not show a smooth progression but rather a certain pendulum-movement, indicating that what is rejected or repressed in one period may come to be in vogue in the next. Such awareness gives a more balanced view of current

fads and fashions, and the ability to see one-sided arguments and formulations in perspective. Third, knowledge of the social and cultural context in which problems arose and answers were sought in the past provides an insight into the dynamics of history which can help us to anticipate likely future developments. These are not the only good reasons for learning about history, but they are sufficient in themselves to justify looking at the origins of our field, and tracing how things evolved.

Although the majority of psychologists work in an applied field, historical accounts of the development of psychological practice are rare. Of the many books on general psychology and its history, some make mention of applied work, but usually in a selective way. As most histories of psychology are of American origin, there tends to be an over-emphasis on developments in the USA. But the same trend towards a one-sided national perspective can be seen too in European histories of applied psychology. For example, the otherwise valuable book by Dorsch (1963) is written almost entirely from a German perspective. Our aim in this chapter is to review developments in the field as a whole, with particular reference to the West

European and American scene. Space does not allow of a country by country account of all that has occurred in work and organizational psychology. Instead we shall focus on key persons, institutions, and events exerting a major influence on the development of the domain, and show how specific features of the environment and of the parent discipline led to the establishment of various areas of application.

For convenience, we will present our account in terms of four periods:

1. Establishing the profession (up to 1945)
2. Post-war expansion and consolidation (until the late 1960s)
3. New directions and reorientation (the late 1960s and 1970s)
4. Later developments.

This division is necessarily artificial, as there are no sharp disjunctions in the course of history, but it enables us to illustrate the interaction between the emergence of new problems which pose a challenge to a scientific discipline, the responses made to these challenges through the application of existing knowledge or through the development of new *concepts* and techniques, and the opportunities which this interactive process provides to establish distinctive domains of skills and practice.

We therefore begin our review of each period by outlining the *challenges and opportunities* that characterized those years. Then we describe the initiatives taken by psychologists in *response* to these challenges, followed by an account of the *theories and methods* they used or developed specifically for this purpose. Within each period, particularly the first, which covers nearly half a century, there was a sequence of challenges and responses, but it is not practicable in this chapter to give a detailed description of the subperiods. We hope, nevertheless, that we have been able to highlight all major new developments that took place in each of our four time periods.

In the final section of the chapter, we examine the *dynamics* of the history we have portrayed, by asking certain questions: Why did the psychology of work and organization develop in the way it did? What role was played by significant persons, institutions, and events? What favourable circumstances and felicitous choices led to particular lines of development and what opportunities appear to have been missed? What are the dilemmas and conflicts that confront W&O psychologists? And what lessons can be learned from the past? Posing these questions gives an insight into the relationship between theory and practice and between science and society. With these in mind, our concluding paragraphs assess the present state of the field, the problems facing its practitioners and the directions it may take in the future, but, in contrast with the detached, historical position taken in the previous sections, we end by giving our personal opinion of the discipline now and in the years to come.

ESTABLISHING THE PROFESSION

Prelude

When scientific psychology became established as an independent discipline in the latter part of the last century, for the founding fathers like Wilhelm Wundt and his associates the primary task was to build a sound body of knowledge of mental life based on laboratory experimentation. Until this could be achieved, they considered that it would be premature and inappropriate to seek to apply the subject to practical problems in the world at large. However, this view was not endorsed by members of the next generation of psychologists, for example, Münsterberg (1912) who wrote that, just as the practice of medicine did not await the completion of anatomical and physiological knowledge, neither should *psychotechnics* (the application of psychology to practical problems) await the coming-of-age of basic psychology. Even before the turn of the century, pioneering work by a few individuals was preparing the ground for the development of applied psychology in a number of spheres, particularly education and industry. Thus, in 1889 L.P. Patrizi had founded a Laboratory of Work Psychology at Modena in Italy; systematic studies of individual differences by Francis Galton (1883) in England, and by James McKeen Cattell (1890) in the United States had laid the foundations of psychological testing;

and psychophysiological investigations of fatigue and workload had been carried out by Mosso (1890/1904) in Italy and Kraepelin (1896, 1902) in Germany. In addition, American engineers like Taylor (1911) and Gilbreth (1911) were developing the principles of "scientific management" in the interests of promoting industrial efficiency. It was evident as the 20th century got under way that psychologists were turning their attention to applications of their discipline. What was it about this period that led them in this direction?

Challenges and opportunities

The emergence of a new field of practice has to be understood against the background of the social and cultural conditions prevailing at the time and, above all else, the last part of the 19th century was an expansionist period. Scientific exploration, colonial expansion, the growth of industry and commerce, accompanied by the employment of new sources of energy, the invention of new machinery, the development of new means of transport and communications, led to material progress, while, in the realm of ideas, the ferment caused by Charles Darwin's (1859) theory of evolution challenged conventional beliefs about the immutability of the animal species. At the same time, social reformers campaigned against the exploitation of factory labour and pressed for better public health measures and educational provision. By 1900 compulsory education was established in most industrialized countries.

Awareness that progress in these directions derived from advances in the natural and biological sciences, it was natural to look to the new mental sciences to assist in achieving improvements in society as a whole and in dealing with specific problems. Thus, in the sphere of education, as the intellectual demands on school pupils increased, the need to be able to differentiate between, and to make special provision for, those of differing mental ability became apparent. Alfred Binet's construction of a scale to measure mental age resulted from his appointment to a committee on special classes in schools (Binet & Simon, 1905). In industry, progressive mechanisation and rationalization of work put new demands on the workers, as did the advent of typewriters and telecommunication in the office environment.

Whereas entry to an occupation had previously been a matter of sons following their fathers and daughters their mothers into particular forms of employment, the problem of determining individuals' vocational abilities arose as well as of their performance on the job, which had to meet higher requirements, since the introduction of scientific management. In the realm of transport, the new methods of road and rail travel and, by the end of this first period under review, of air traffic, led to numerous accidents, many of which, it was felt, related to the alertness and speed of reactions of the drivers and pilots concerned.

Another area of application was advertising and its effectiveness, pioneered by an American student of Wundt's, W.D. Scott (1903, 1908, 1911) following an approach by the advertising manager of a chain of magazines asking him to undertake research on the topic. This was later to develop into a subdiscipline in its own right under the heading of marketing and market research and, as such, is referred to only in passing in this chapter. Similarly, other branches of applied psychology—clinical, educational and criminological—originated from early work by enterprising psychologists who, unlike modern specialists, did not confine their interests to one sphere of application. For example, Münsterberg (1907, 1909) had written on psychological applications in the law courts and in the classroom before he published his book on the psychology of industrial efficiency in 1913.

By the outbreak of World War I which, like World War II a quarter of a century later, was to give a great impetus to the subject, "psychotechnical" applications of psychology were well in place, although on a small scale. In Europe, the embattled countries sought the aid of psychologists in selecting men for specific occupations such as telegraph operators, "hydrophone" operators (engaged in submarine detection), and so on, but the impact of their work was limited and psychologists themselves were few in number. It was only after the United States entered the war in 1917 that the potential of psychology for dealing with practical problems was demonstrated in a dramatic fashion. A Committee on the Psychological Examination of Recruits, set up by the American Psychological Association, devised

group tests specifically for this purpose and in less than a year about 1.7 million men had been tested and recruits for military service selected on the basis of test scores.

In Britain, attention focused on another wartime problem, that of the hours of work and productivity of women workers in the munitions factories who had replaced the male workers who had joined up. The factories attempted to increase production by extending hours of work to the point where, due to fatigue and associated health problems, there was a falling-off rather than a rise in output and a shortfall in the supply of shells to the front. It was a government-funded body in this instance, the Health of Munition Workers' Committee, that was established to investigate the problem and which enlisted the aid of psychologists in carrying out its task (Hearnshaw, 1964; Smith, 1945). In Germany, too, psychologists were engaged in problems in munition factories, arising from the replacement of men by unqualified women (Jaeger & Staueble, 1981).

After the War, industrial expansion and the return of ex-service personnel to civilian employment extended the opportunities for psychologists. Interest in the use of psychological tests not only for selection but also for educational and vocational guidance persisted, as did that in working conditions and in factors affecting industrial output. It was from a study of the effects on productivity of variations in the level of illumination, carried out in the Western Electric Company's Hawthorne plant near Chicago, that the further investigations derived that showed the famous "Hawthorne effect" (Mayo, 1933). These alerted psychologists and others to the influence of social and group factors on workers' attitudes and performance and stimulated the growth of what was to become known as the "Human Relations Movement" in later years.

With the economic depression of the 1930s, opportunities for industrial and other applications of psychology declined, although there was continuing activity in the field of personnel selection and the study of the working environment. In Germany, the Nazi regime and the political and racial persecution that accompanied it dealt a heavy blow to psychology. Many of the best minds left and contributed significantly to developments elsewhere, for example Kurt Lewin in the United States. Ideological influences tended to dominate the theories of those who remained under the Nazi yoke. On the other hand, the rebuilding of the German armed forces after the Nazis took over gave new opportunities to military psychologists, the training and status of whom were determined by law in 1937 (Geuter, 1984/1992; Smith, 1945).

World War II presented many challenges to psychologists and marked another period of acceleration in the applied field, especially for the Western Allies. In addition to the problems of selection and classification of recruits so that the personnel of the armed services were assigned to tasks commensurate with their abilities, the war led to increased study of human–machine interactions related to questions of the optimal design of control displays in ships, aircraft, radar detection, and other new equipment. Psychologists were also consulted about problems of morale, motivation, leadership, and cooperation in groups, and the effects of propaganda and "psychological warfare". However, in the countries occupied by Nazi Germany the war meant a period of relative stagnation in psychology (Baumgarten, 1949).

As a result of the developments outlined in this section, by 1945 the practical contributions that psychology could make to human affairs were recognized in many quarters. Within a period of four decades from its origins as an experimental science and the cautious approach of Wundt and other pioneers towards its application, an increasing number of problems in society had become formulated as *psychological problems* that could no longer be dealt with in the traditional way, but called for a scientific approach.

Responses to these challenges

Reference has been made already to some of the key individuals who were instrumental in applying psychology in the spheres of education, industry, the law courts, and so on. Early work on psychological testing in schools was conducted not only by Binet (1895) in France but also by Wittmer (1896) in the USA, Ebbinghaus (1897) in Germany, and Spearman (1904) in England. The first attempts at vocational guidance occurred not much later and the first bureaus for this purpose were opened almost simultaneously, and probably

independently, in the USA (Parsons in Boston, 1908) and in Belgium (Christiaens in Brussels, 1909). Elsewhere—in England, France, Germany, and Spain—the newly established employment exchanges gradually began to take psychological factors into consideration in recommending suitable employment to school-leavers.

Lahy in France was one of the first psychologists to respond to the challenge of selecting workers for jobs influenced by developing mechanization and technology. He applied tests to typists in 1905 and to railway and tramway drivers in 1908 (Lahy, 1927). Other vocational aptitude tests were developed for telephone operators, navigating officers on large steamers, and motormen on Boston streetcars in the applied section of Münsterberg's Harvard laboratory. Münsterberg saw the role of the applied psychologist as analogous to that of the engineer, an approach which was encapsulated in the term *psychotechnics*, first proposed by William Stern (1903), another pioneering influence in child and "differential" psychology (Stern, 1900) and in the sphere of the psychology of testimony. After Münsterberg had published his influential handbook on psychotechnics (1914) in the German language, the term became very popular on the mainland of Europe, but never gained wide acceptance in English usage. Though Münsterberg had a wide range of applications in view, the term gradually became almost synonymous with industrial psychology.

It was not only academic psychologists who responded to the challenges of applying psychology to practical affairs, but members of other professions such as engineers, teachers, school doctors, and psychiatrists, who took from psychology whatever they deemed useful for the problems they encountered in their fields of practice. A good example of its use by an enterprising engineer is that of Georg Schlesinger, professor of machine tool engineering and industrial sciences at the Technical University in Berlin and champion of rationalization of the workshop. As early as 1912, he had begun to experiment with personnel selection techniques, and in 1918 he created a "Workstation for Industrial Psychotechnics" in that institution. He hired Walther Moede, another of Wundt's former students, to give short

courses for engineers on selection procedures and other aspects of personnel management (Hinrichs, 1981; Wilpert, 1990). The result was that, within a few years, no less than 74 German firms had installed psychotechnical "test stations" in which academic psychologists played hardly any part. This soon led to a controversy between psychologists and engineers about competence in administering tests (Jaeger & Staeuble, 1981), disputes about which were to recur many times and in different places in subsequent years and act as a strong impetus to psychologists to professionalize as an applied science.

In some other countries, for example the USSR, engineers also played a large part in the development of psychotechnics. Elsewhere, it was academic psychologists who took the initiative, as when R.M. Yerkes, as president of the American Psychological Association, set in motion the large-scale testing of army recruits in World War I which we mentioned earlier, and W.D. Scott, after contributing notably to a classification and placement programme for the expanding American army, founded the first successful psychological consultancy firm in that country in 1919. A British example is that of C.S. Myers, whose original training was in medicine but who founded and directed the Cambridge Psychological Laboratory before serving in the war as "Consulting Psychologist to the British Armies in France". After the war he turned his attention to applied psychology, establishing the National Institute of Industrial Psychology (NIIP), after two years of preparation, in London in 1921. The NIIP, together with the Industrial Fatigue Research Board (later the Industrial Health Research Board) set up in 1918 as successor to the wartime Health of Munition Workers Committee, was the mainstay of developments in industrial psychology in Britain in the interwar years (Frisby, 1970; Shimmin & Wallis, 1994; Welch & Myers, 1932; Yeokes, 1991).

It is not possible here to detail how the "psychotechnical movement" progressed in all countries of the European continent. Noteworthy is the intensive international exchange within Europe which came about soon after the War. In 1920, Edouard Claparède, the most prominent Swiss psychologist of his day and founder of an Institute for Vocational Guidance at Geneva,

convened an International Conference of Psycho-techniques. From this gathering emerged the forerunner of the present International Association of Applied Psychology. During the following 15 years, seven other international meetings were held: at Barcelona (1921), Milan (1922), Paris (1927), Utrecht (1928), Barcelona (1930), Moscow (1931), and Prague (1934). These locations and the much less frequent international conferences devoted to general psychology (only five in the whole interwar period) show the dominant role played by applied psychology in the development and spread of psychology in Europe at that time. From 1955 onward the conferences were continued as International Congresses of Applied Psychology and the term psychotechnics fell into disuse and was gradually abandoned.

This formation of an international network was another sign of the movement towards pro-fessionalization, which had begun with the estab-lishment of national associations around the turn of the century. Thus, the American Psychological Association (APA) was founded in 1892, the Société Française de Psychologie in 1901, the British Psychological Society in 1902, and the Deutsche Gesellschaft fur experimentelle Psy-chologie in 1904 ("experimentelle" was dropped from the title in 1929). Other countries followed suit and, by the 1930s, nearly all European countries had a national association. In some, for example the Netherlands, special associations for practising psychologists were formed as well. Likewise, several journals devoted to applied psychology were founded in the first quarter of this century to complement those established for general or experimental psychology at an earlier date.

From the 1920s onwards, university chairs in psychology and/or the inclusion of the basics of psychological practice in degree courses in psy-chology were further indications of the growing trend towards professionalization. Whereas the subject had been studied previously as a special-ism within philosophy, attracting relatively few students and offering few vocational opportunities outside academia, it now became the training ground for professional practice in a number of applied areas.

Not surprisingly, one of the major concerns of the professional psychological associations was to protect and distinguish their members from those with no qualifications in the subject and to suppress charlatanism. The possibility of develop-ing standards that would differentiate between self-made practitioners and qualified pro-fessionals was discussed by American psychol-ogists as early as 1911 and, in 1915, the APA passed a resolution on this issue (Napoli, 1981). As we mentioned earlier, in Germany there was contention between engineers and psychologists in the 1920s about their "right to practise" and similar disputes elsewhere (for the Netherlands see Veldkamp & Van Drunen, 1988). In ensuing years and, indeed, right up to the present time, attempts have been made to strengthen the pro-fessional status of psychology and psychologists by seeking legal protection of their work and registration of their title, and through organizing themselves as a profession, with an ethical code of practice and procedures for dealing with pro-fessional misconduct, rather than functioning solely as a scientific, learned society.

Despite such attempts, work and organizational psychology has never become the exclusive domain of psychologists. As the areas of practice extended and the presenting problems became more complex, it was evident, particularly during and after World War II, that they were amenable to multidisciplinary approaches. Progressively, psychoanalysts, specialists in industrial medicine, engineers and members of other professions worked in the same broad area as psychologists, sometimes to the latter's dismay. In the next and following sections of this chapter, we shall discuss the impact of these trends on theories and practice in our field.

Theoretical approaches and methods of working

The experimental methods of the psychological laboratories of the period shaped the first "tests" employed by the pioneers of applied psychology. Apparatus designed to discover general laws of human perception and responses was now used to assess individual differences (Van Strien, 1997). In accordance with the prevailing "philosophy of consciousness", suitability for a job was con-ceived in terms of separate, elementary functions

and sometimes fitness for a specific task was seen as dependent solely on one function. Hence, Münsterberg used reaction time as the sole indicator of suitability for driving tramcars. However, in the case of telephone operators, he identified 14 separate functions (attention, memory, speed, accuracy, etc.) in the job and used eight different tests to measure them. To decide which of the individuals tested best fitted the demands of a job, the early psychotechnicians used the profiles of test scores on each function and compared them with those of job incumbents. Correlation coefficients only gradually came into use as a basis for prediction in selection procedures (Van Strien, 1994).

For psychomotor skills such as driving, some psychologists advocated using a complex task in testing applicants instead of elementary tests. The chauffeur-cabin, designed by Lahy of Paris, was a realistic mock-up of the actual driving situation which brought him international fame. Seated behind the steering wheel, the test subject had to avoid obstacles projected on a film screen. In the 1920s, a German psychotechnical firm took out a patent for films of this kind for use in driver selection. From these developments a debate arose about the relative merits of the "global" and the "analytic" approach (in which suitability was seen as a composite of separate functions) to selection, but, in the course of time, specially constructed paper and pencil tests and performance tests superseded the use of apparatus in this context.

Following the pioneering work of Binet in testing schoolchildren, the intelligence test in various forms gradually assumed the position of the psychologists' most powerful tool, especially after the mass testing of recruits by the American army in World War I and the ensuing debate about the intellectual age of immigrants. Interest in intelligence as a basic factor was further enhanced by the controversy that arose in the 1920s about the possible effects of heredity versus environmental influences on intelligence (Block & Dworkin, 1976). Theoretical arguments about the nature of intelligence surrounded attempts to measure it. Thus, as early as 1904, the British psychologist Charles Spearman contended that the score on any test reflected the operation of a general factor "g" and one specific to the test itself, the correlations

that are obtained between scores on several tests deriving from a single underlying general function. This assertion provoked much controversy. Thorndike (1927), for example, rejected the concept of a "general factor", but Thurstone (1938), using his method of "factor analysis" considered his results did not preclude it (Murray, 1983). The debate, together with the growing statistical sophistication that accompanied it, particularly in the UK and the USA, resulted in greater sensitivity to the psychometric properties of tests among psychologists, including the importance of validity and reliability and the availability of group norms in assessing the significance to be attached to test results. In these countries, a number of other psychometric tests were also developed aimed at measuring aptitudes, interests, and personality attributes, for example the test of personal values presented by Allport and Vernon (1931).

On the continent of Europe, notably in the German-speaking world, development took another direction (Hermann, 1966). In the aftermath of the slaughter of World War I, there was a loss of faith in the technical and social progress of the previous period, particularly among the younger generation of psychologists. Natural science methodology, with its aim of discovering elementary properties and basic laws, lost its supremacy to the deeper understanding the *Geisteswissenschaftliche* approach promised to offer. In the practice of personnel selection and vocational guidance, the old intelligence and performance tests were preserved, but they were supplemented by new kinds of test that purported to capture the deeper structure of personality, namely expression and projection tests. The role model of the *engineer*, that had inspired the pioneers of psychotechnics, gave way around 1930 to that of the *diagnostician*, who sees separate phenomena as indicators of a deeper, underlying pattern in the way that medical practitioners view the symptoms of their patients. Many typologies of personality and character evolved during this period to serve as a conceptual framework for the diagnosis of the person as an incumbent or prospective incumbent of a job.

This new "holistic" approach was taken up and widely used by the psychological services of the Nazi-German *Wehrmacht*. The assessment centres

in which individuals were observed performing complex, and often stressful, individual and group tasks (Simoneit, 1943; Wyatt & Teuber, 1944) attracted the attention of military psychologists elsewhere in Europe and in Japan. In Britain, the War Office Selection Boards established in 1942, in which psychiatrists as well as psychologists participated, were based on this German model (Vernon & Parry, 1949) and their approach, in turn, was copied by the Office of Strategic Services in the USA (OSS-Assessment Staff, 1948). The validity and reliability of the quasi real-life situations used and the concomitant "clinical" overall appraisal of candidates later came under critical scrutiny (Kelly & Fiske, 1951) but the multiple assessment methods of selection in use in the present-day Assessment Centres, although different in form and content, can trace their origin to these war-time practices.

Another new development was the growth of interest in designing jobs or changing jobs, tools and instruments to fit the psychological and physiological capacities of the workers. This activity, originally termed "object-psychotechnics", had been undertaken by psychologists in various countries before the war, usually apart from, but sometimes alongside, their work in personnel selection. During the 1930s, for example, this was the case in the Psychological Department of the Dutch Postal Services (Biegel, 1938). The subject, known in the United States as Human Engineering and in Europe as the multi-disciplinary field of Ergonomics, a term coined by the British psychologist Murrell (Murrell, 1965; Edholm & Murrell, 1974), really "took off" during World War II, when psychologists working for the armed services were presented with the task of designing equipment for human use. Their efforts were directed, in particular, to improving the lay-out of controls and instrument panels in ships and aircraft, in the course of which the concept of the human operator as an integral part of a man–machine system was developed (Craik, 1947, 1948). The further expansion of the field and the ways in which this work contributed subsequently to a new development in general psychology—the cognitive revolution—is described in later sections.

In industry, the ideas of Taylor and Gilbreth

concerning the rationalization of production had become the dominant principle governing the organization of work and the tasks of the operators, whose individual performance was to be controlled on a strictly economic contract basis. This focus on the individual worker as the key to efficiency was shared by the psychotechnicians and industrial psychologists who sought to assess the capabilities of individuals and their reactions to specific stimuli under various conditions, as in a laboratory, so as to achieve an effective use of human resources. The results of the Hawthorne studies, therefore, to which we referred earlier, which showed the influence of social-psychological factors in the workplace, not only challenged the advocates of a scientific management approach but also the individualistic perspective of many applied psychologists. Although the "Hawthorne effect" (mentioned previously), whereby becoming the subject of special attention appears to have a stronger motivating effect than an instrumental incentive, had been observed earlier in some British studies (Shimmin, 1986), and the conclusions of the Hawthorne investigators have been questioned later on (Baritz, 1960; Carey, 1967; Gillespie, 1991), the impact of these studies was far-reaching. Both within and outside the social sciences, the attention they received led to a "paradigm shift" in which the social aspects of work got priority over individual factors.

The study of group phenomena received another impetus from Kurt Lewin's field theory and his use of groups to bring about changed attitudes. His studies of group dynamics (1947, 1948) were to influence the direction taken by the emergent interest in organizational psychology. Focus on the small group as a unit of analysis was further stimulated after the war by the publication of far-reaching studies made by the research division of the US War Department's Information and Education Division, which showed the key role played by primary group relations in maintaining morale and efficiency (Stouffer et al., 1949). In these studies, just as in the Human Relations Movement, there has been a blending of sociological, psychological, and psychoanalytic lines of thought, and an input from some management theorists.

POST-WAR EXPANSION AND CONSOLIDATION

With the ending of the war in Europe in 1945 and with Japan in 1946, the protagonists were faced with the restoration of a peace-time economy in their countries and, in many instances, with rebuilding and reconstructing their towns and cities, which had been devastated by the ravages of war. The United States, although not suffering the physical devastation experienced elsewhere, shared with her Allies the problem of re-establishing war veterans and ex-prisoners of war in civilian life, a situation which was compounded in Europe by numbers of displaced persons and refugees unable or unwilling to return to their countries of origin. It was a period that presented great opportunities for psychologists who, as we have seen, had demonstrated their ability to apply their expertise to war-time problems, to expand and consolidate their activities in a number of directions. What was the nature of these opportunities?

Challenges and opportunities in the aftermath of World War II

The structure of work and society after the war was shaped not only by the technological advances made that led to new jobs, new products, new forms of communication and transport, etc., but also by people's changed expectations and aspirations. For many, these focused on the concept of a more egalitarian society without the religious, class, or occupational divisions they had known pre-war. How this was to be achieved had been considered by a number of prominent individuals in the countries concerned, even during the war, and gave rise subsequently to what became known as the "welfare state" (i.e. state-subsidized health care, social services, unemployment benefit, and so on) in Britain and the Netherlands, for example, and to experiments in industrial democracy and codetermination in Norway, the former West Germany, and elsewhere.

Another factor was the ending of colonialism and the granting of independence to their former overseas colonies on which the European trading nations had relied for raw materials for their exports. This led to an increasingly unfavourable balance of trade with the USA and the declaration by Secretary of State George Marshall in 1947 that, unless given extensive financial aid by America, Europe was in danger of "economic, social and political deterioration of a very grave character". As a result, 1948 saw the launch of Marshall Aid (and the creation of a special organization—OECD—to administer it) which promoted visits by European productivity teams to the USA and led to an orientation towards American management methods. In the same year, Czechoslovakia became the latest state of Eastern Europe to come under communist control, resulting in an "iron curtain" dividing not only occupied Germany but also Europe as a whole. This heralded the Cold War between the United States and her allies, on the one hand, and countries dominated by the Soviet Union, on the other, that was to prevail over the next decades.

The resulting defensive alliance of NATO, through which the majority of Western European countries were linked to the US, was another mediating influence of American ideas and practice, not only among work psychologists associated with the armed forces but also in academic circles. In the United States much of the basic research on human capacities and limitations in relation to the design of equipment by American university psychologists was undertaken on behalf of the Office of Naval Research and similar bodies. In Europe, too, many commissioned research projects were conducted under contract to the military. NATO to this end had established a special Human Factors Advisory Panel (European Productivity Agency, 1958).

Throughout the 1950s and 1960s openings and opportunities for industrial and work psychologists widened considerably. The need to increase industrial productivity in the post-war period of reconstruction and revival, when labour resources were scarce and people's expectations and aspirations were changing, focused attention on the motivation of workers, on the design of jobs, on styles and patterns of leadership, and on participation in change processes. Research by psychologists on both sides of the Atlantic showed the

limitations of traditional views of economic factors and the rationalization of work as key determinants of performance. It reflected the emergent interest in the quality of life in general, and the quality of working life in particular, that began to gather momentum during this period and which became an international movement in the early 1970s.

New technologies, an associated demand for new skills, changes in the composition of the workforce in which women played an increasing part and, later, an influx of immigrant and "guest" workers, called for an enhanced contribution from psychologists in both the selection and training of personnel for new expanding industrial plants and in the growing service sector. Management training and development became important areas of concern, as did the nature of organizations, to the study of which other social scientists as well as psychologists were to make important contributions. It was evident that only to a very limited extent were psychologists being asked for "more of the same" services they had provided formerly, but that the new social, technological, and intellectual climate demanded largely new approaches, new kinds of expertise, and a much broader scope of activities under the rubric of work psychology. In these, as in other spheres of activity, exchange of information and personnel and collaboration across national boundaries was greatly facilitated by the advances in means of communication and of travel that occurred in the post-war era. Despite the Cold War atmosphere characterizing relations between the major political powers of East and West, it was an exciting time for social theorists, technical innovators, and creative artists alike, with social reform and scientific advances clearly on the horizon.

Responses to these challenges

In response to these developments, there was an upsurge of interest in and provision for the study of social and behavioral sciences. From the late 1940s onwards, throughout Europe, psychology expanded considerably as increasing numbers of students were attracted to the subject, new academic departments and training programmes were started, and independent research groups set up. Although its rate of growth was linear, rather than

showing the exponential growth of psychology as a whole (de Wolff, Shimmin, & de Montmollin, 1981), there was a comparable expansion in work and organizational psychology during this period. Jobs for graduates were plentiful as more industrial and governmental organizations began to employ psychologists, for example in Britain a separate Psychologist Class of the Civil Service was established in 1950. Other work psychologists became consultants, operating either as self-employed individuals or as members of a consulting organization, on a variety of problems such as the design of jobs, the introduction of technological change, selection and training issues, and so on. Requests for assistance of this kind increased with accelerating rates of change and innovation in both the public and private sectors of employment, and organizational consultancy became a recognized employment opening for applied psychologists, although not restricted to this discipline.

The 1960s saw a rapid expansion in research and consultancy assignments related to the structure and functioning of organizations, and the introduction of organizational change. This accompanied a concern with styles and patterns of management (Likert, 1961) and an emphasis on "participation" and "democracy" in the workplace as conducive to effective performance, terms that often signified techniques of communication rather than changes in the way power and control was exercised (Hollway, 1991), but which accorded with the ideology of the time. Managerial behaviour became as much, if not more, the focus of attention as that of shop-floor employees. This new focus was reflected in the development of business schools and management education.

Accompanying and reflecting this expansion of the field was a growth in the professional and institutional organization of work and organizational psychology. For example, in the Netherlands, where there had been fewer than 20 industrial psychologists in 1945, their number rose to 100 at the beginning of the 1960s and to more than 250 by the end of that decade. Membership of the Netherlands Institute of Practising Psychology (NIPP), founded in 1938 by a small group of pioneers, grew from 36 in 1946 to nearly 300 in 1960 (Van Strien, de Wolff, & Takens, 1987).

Even in countries where the political regime was inimical to the development of psychology, the 1950s and 1960s saw the beginning of a forward movement, as in Spain, where Peiro (1985) notes the revival signified by the founding of the Spanish Society of Psychology in 1952 and the creation of a professional School of Psychology and Psychotechnics for postgraduate students in 1953 (see also Peiro & Munduate, 1994). The 12th International Congress of Applied Psychology, held in London in 1956, was attended by some 500 psychologists from 29 different countries and addressed educational, industrial, clinical, and social issues. Since then, according to Lévy-Leboyer (1988), the growth of applied psychology has been spectacular, with worldwide numbers doubling every six years and new fields of activity and application opening every year.

Accompanying this expansion, diversification took place within the different areas of application, with the result that "industrial" was seen by some as too restrictive a label for the range of activities undertaken by practitioners in this field. As Dunnette (1990) points out, this was the title used for the relevant chapter in the Annual Review of Psychology before 1961 but, in that year and subsequently, separate chapters were devoted to personnel management, industrial social psychology, consumer psychology, personnel selection, engineering psychology, and, finally, in 1967, there appeared the first chapter on organizational psychology.

Methods of working ("paradigms of practice")

Personnel selection continued to be one of the main activities of work and organizational psychologists, in many instances drawing on the batteries of tests and psychological procedures developed in military contexts during the war. For example, in Britain, the Civil Service Selection Board adopted assessment methods based on those of the War Office Selection Boards and a composite cognitive test battery constructed by Admiralty psychologists was used by Ministry of Labour psychologists in assessing the work capabilities of disabled individuals referred to Industrial Rehabilitation Units. The approach adopted was in the statistical tradition exemplified by the

work of psychologists such as Thorndike (1949) in the USA and Vernon and Parry (1949) in the UK, underpinned by factor-analytic models of the structure of individual differences and "trait and type" theories of personality. But, in the Netherlands and elsewhere on the mainland of Europe, apart from military psychologists, who became acquainted with Anglo-Saxon selection procedures through their contacts within NATO, the clinical approach to selection prevailed for many years after the war. Attempts were made to obtain a comprehensive, intuitive understanding of the personality of applicants through elaborate psychodiagnostic interviews, observation tests, and projective techniques that were very time-consuming. It was not until the late 1950s to mid-1960s that the statistical approach was adopted more widely, largely influenced by developing links with American psychologists and the widespread use of American textbooks (de Wolff et al., 1981). The clinical approach, however, was not set on one side entirely and continues in use in various places, notably in many of the assessment centres for appraising management potential (see later).

Alongside concern with selection, increased attention was given to training, not only for the skills required in the use of new technologies but also those entailed in the supervision and management of employees. For the latter, schemes under the general title of Training Within Industry (TWI) aimed at promoting a new, and less authoritarian, supervisory style, were undertaken in several European countries, supported by Marshall Aid funds, although the involvement of psychologists in these programmes varied. In Britain, for example, they were conducted mainly by industrial trainers and tended to be disregarded by psychologists. Experimental studies of learning and the acquisition of skill, e.g. the effectiveness of respectively part, progressive part, or whole learning, were utilized in developing methods of teaching both young and older workers to perform new tasks, accompanied by a growing awareness of the importance of systematic job analysis and the techniques available to undertake it (Blum & Naylor, 1968). A powerful stimulus to psychological work in this area were theories of human behaviour emerging from the experimental studies of the Medical Research Council Applied Psychology Unit, Cambridge, such as those of Mackworth (1956) and Broadbent (1958, 1961). During the 1960s, there was an upsurge of interest in programmed instruction, based on behaviourist principles, and the use of teaching machines by commercial and industrial organizations. Although, for a variety of reasons, this did not become as widespread as at first seemed likely (Robertson & Cooper, 1983), by focusing attention on the importance of clarifying the objectives of training programmes and of ensuring that effective feedback is given to trainees about their learning responses, programmed instruction has had a considerable influence on approaches to training as a whole.

Managerial and leadership training had different roots and reflected a number of American influences, differentially taken up by European work psychologists. It was directed towards increasing an individual's awareness of the social processes occurring within groups and organizations in order to bring about personal and organizational change. Kurt Lewin's field theory and his method of "group dynamics training", based at the Research Centre for Group Dynamics at Michigan, was one strand in this development. Another was the sensitivity or T-group training run by National Training Laboratories, of which the first was held at Bethel, Maine in 1947. Both contributed to the concept of intervening in, changing, and developing organizations, which, under the heading of organization development (OD), acquired its own momentum and identity during the late 1960s, with adherents and practitioners not confined to psychologists (Bennis, Benne, & Chin, 1969).

Links with both the above centres were formed in Britain by members of the Tavistock Institute of Human Relations, itself a post-war development, but its theoretical orientations were more eclectic, with psycho-analytic underpinnings. In terms of paradigms of practice, the Tavistock Institute became noted for a number of innovations, such as its pioneering studies in the Glacier Metal Company where Jaques (1951), as the first full-time organization consultant to work with a UK firm, laid the foundations of the action-research model

that has characterized the Institute's approach to organizational change ever since.

Its most well-known investigation of this period, however, was of the human effects of technological change in a coal-mine, which led to the discovery of self-regulating work groups and from which the concept of an organization as an open socio-technical system evolved (Trist, Higgin, Murray, & Pollock, 1963). This was to stimulate research and experiments in work and organizational design world-wide in the following decades. For example, an extensive programme of work restructuring was undertaken at Philips Industries in the Netherlands using the sociotechnical paradigm, while in Norway it led to a major series of "experiments in industrial democracy" under the auspices of the Oslo Work Research Institute (Emery & Thorsrud, 1969).

NEW DIRECTIONS AND REORIENTATION

By the end of the 1960s the Welfare State was well-established in most advanced industrial nations and the Western world had achieved a high level of prosperity. There were, however, signs of unease about the causes and consequences of this wealth, particularly among the young, including the increased, and increasing, number of psychology students. It was evident too that the economic structure of society was changing from one based largely on manufacturing industry to a "post-industrial" era characterized by an expanding service sector and a growth in non-profit making institutions. Industrial psychologists, and those taking the specialized degree courses in the subject that had been introduced in many universities, were confronted with a debate about their allegiance in a world of increasingly conflicting social forces. The nature of the new problems and opportunities that faced them in this period and the ways in which they responded form the subject of this section.

Challenges and opportunities in a world of conflicts and contradictions

The years in question saw a transition from the optimism of the previous decade about the ability of human beings to improve the economic and social order with the aid of science and technology to doubt, dissent, and uncertainty about the uses and abuses of this knowledge. Radical critiques of established power-relations, associated with perceived inequity in the distribution of the benefits of the newly acquired prosperity, and fed by a wave of neo-Marxist thinking which became fashionable in universities and among opinion leaders in the wider society, led to the challenging of traditional assumptions about the industrial and social order. Suspicion of and antagonism to the "military-industrial complex" was strong, enhanced by controversy over the war in Vietnam and the plight of young Americans drafted to fight there. At the same time, it was evident that the balance of power between nations at a global level was changing, illustrated by the outbreak of the Arab–Israeli war in 1973 and the ensuing energy crisis when Arab oil producers cut oil supplies to their Western customers. On all fronts, previously held assumptions were being challenged.

For social scientists in general, but psychologists in particular, the charge that they were the servants of power was voiced in America by Baritz (1960). Psychological testing came under fire in the USA on a number of grounds in the early 1960s. For example, intelligence testing was accused of putting minority groups at a disadvantage; and personality tests and confidential reports to employers on individuals who had no access to these reports were regarded as an intrusion of privacy. In Europe, criticisms of this kind were often reflected in the student protest movements of the late 1960s and early 1970s which, although occurring in differing situations and circumstances, had at their root rejection of established authority and the desire for "power-sharing" and participation in decision making. There was a naive idealization of the situation in the Eastern European "socialist countries", and an avid interest in the Yugoslavian model of workers' participation.

The same pressures and challenges to the "managerial prerogative" were also expressed in business and industry, linked with demands for equal opportunities in the workplace, legal protection against unfair dismissal, and similar measures. All this contributed to a climate of opinion

in Western Europe which, on the one hand, encouraged greater interference by the state in the form of employment legislation and regulation and, on the other, of many experimental ventures in joint consultation, codetermination and the "humanization" of work in which psychologists were closely involved.

Within universities, work psychologists faced challenges of two kinds in justifying their specialization. For the growing numbers of psychology students, clinical psychology had the greatest appeal and the number of those opting to take industrial psychology dropped considerably. This was difficult for their teachers, many of them newly appointed, who had to convince students that interest in the problems of working life did not lead inevitably to collusion in exploiting and manipulating the least powerful members of society. They found too that it was no longer sufficient to be successful practitioners looking primarily to their clients for approval and validation of their activities, but that, if they were to gain respect in academia, they had to demonstrate that the theoretical and methodological bases of their applied work were as sound as those of more established academic fields. Many found the differing criteria of their academic and client publics impossible to meet simultaneously, so that a gulf developed between theory and practice. For some, the dilemma was resolved by teaching in the management and business schools, which also expanded considerably at this time, in which the prevailing emphasis was on the practical relevance of the subjects taught rather than on their theoretical foundations.

The contradictory and conflicting pressures in society as a whole were mirrored in the industrial and business environment. On the one hand, there was progressive rationalization and bureaucratization of enterprises, involving take-overs, mergers and the growth of large-scale, multinational organizations, accompanied by an increasing emphasis on profit, which led to the loss of jobs and the closing down of plants with an insufficient return on investments. On the other hand, there was the demand for the overcoming of *alienation* and for the *humanization* of work, which led to an intensification of experiments in participation and job-enlargement and enrichment, which in the

1970s broadened into an international movement for the "quality of working life", spearheaded by social scientists and production engineers (Davis & Cherns, 1975).

In the realm of practice, industrial psychologists found that they could no longer act unquestioningly on behalf of management as their predecessors had done, but that they were put under pressure to take sides and, preferably, to take the side of the least powerful. Some, impressed by the economic success of Japan, thought that industrial relations should be remodelled on the Japanese style of management; others looked to the various forms of codetermination that had emerged in Europe. But psychologists, who traditionally were perceived as concerned with individuals rather than with collectives and as understanding little of the legal/political nature of plant bargaining, could claim no unique expertise in the field of industrial relations. In the field of industrial relations and industrial democracy they soon found themselves working alongside, or in competition with, other specialists undertaking similar assignments who might or might not have had a training in the social sciences. This was, for example, clearly the case in the international project for the study of industrial democracy in Europe (IDE, 1981).

By the end of the 1970s, there was another change in the social climate. Much of the turbulence and protest that had marked the beginning of the decade had abated and there was a shift of emphasis towards individualism. The "culture of narcissism" (Lasch, 1979) emerged, with scope for personal freedom and self-actualization being accorded priority. In some countries this was reflected in a resurgence of the political right, for example as in the election of the Thatcher government in Britain in 1979.

Responses to these challenges

An initial response to the foregoing events was a broadening and diversification of the field, extending further the trends that had become apparent in the 1960s. Formal recognition of this development was signalled in the United States by Division 14 of the American Psychological Association when, in 1973, it changed its name to Division of Industrial and Organizational Psychology (instead of the Divison of Industrial Psychology as for-

merly). Elsewhere, work and organizational psychology (W&O), or a similar title, came into general use. It not only symbolized the transition from an industrial to a post-industrial society, mentioned earlier, and the associated involvement of psychologists in non-industrial enterprises,but it also had the advantage of conveying a less "oppressive" image of the subject to critical students who were wary of its former concentration on traditional industry.

In different nations, the ways in which the field developed varied, as did the density of W&O psychologists. In countries where personnel selection was already a strongly established sphere of activity among psychologists, such as the USA and the Netherlands, it retained its position as an important part of the domain alongside newer areas of activity such as OD, conflict resolution, and job and organizational design. The Scandinavian countries became noted for innovatory experiments in the humanization of work, particularly the widely publicized static-assembly methods developed by the Volvo company in Sweden, as well as for the promotion of industrial democracy which was supported by appropriate labour legislation. In Eastern European socialist countries, where loyalty to the party was often a more important selection criterion than personal aptitude, and where management still operated on traditional hierarchical principles, ergonomics was often the major activity of work psychologists. In fact, according to Bures (1991, p. 9), Czechoslovakia was the only socialist country that gave political approval for psychological diagnostics on the ground that, in a socialist society, social relations were not antagonistic, whereas in a capitalist society psychological selection is a tool of intensifying the exploitation of workers "and serves the capitalist exclusively".

The new focus on organizations as an area of interest led not only to a variety of studies of the effects of organizational variables on the behaviour of individuals, but also to the study of the characteristics of organizations as such and of their interaction with their (increasingly turbulent) environment. A good example of the latter are the studies of the Aston Group (Pugh & Hickson, 1976).

The extending boundaries of the field and

concomitant overlapping of interests with other disciplines, the growth of multidisciplinary approaches to organizational problems and the emergence of new job titles such as "organizational consultant", "management trainer", and the like, led some psychologists to identify with their field of practice rather than with their parent discipline. For these practitioners, the relevant professional organization was that representing their particular domain, which they joined in preference to a professional psychological association. There was also much discussion and debate about the ethical principles guiding psychological consultancy of all kinds.

In some countries, like the Netherlands, this led to the formulation of a new ethical code, in which the rights of clients were better protected and the social responsibility of psychologists was emphasized (Van Strien, 1976). However, in Italy, where the strikes and riots in industry and the universities in 1969 had led to the dissolution of both the Italian Psychological Society (Societá Italiana di Psicologia Scientifica) and the Association of Italian Work Psychologists (Associazione Italiana per la Psicologia del Lavoro), only the former was re-established later (in 1973) and opportunities for industrial psychologists remained restricted (Spaltro, 1980). Elsewhere, psychological associations, which had often functioned more as learned societies than as professional bodies, began to address professional issues such as how to protect members of the public and psychologists from spurious practitioners and dubious procedures. This was attempted in many instances by means of a professional register or other form of chartering and by limiting the use of the title "psychologist" to those with recognized qualifications in the subject.

The development of theories and methods (paradigms of practice)

Although the work of the pioneers of industrial psychology and of the succeeding generation had been guided by theoretical and methodological assumptions, it was only in the third generation that theory-development became (at least in some quarters) a goal in itself. In his introduction to his 1976 *Handbook of Industrial and Organisational Psychology*, Dunnette (p.8) observed that, where-

as in 1950, "practice was technique-oriented and cookbookish", it was now "emerging from the knowledge base developed out of research and theory". He saw theory as less well developed than research methodology, but as nevertheless displaying signs of "maturity in the form of increasing rigor" (Dunnette, 1976, p.8). Summarizing the development from industrial psychology to (work and) organizational psychology since the 1960s, Drenth (1987, p.267) too notes not only a diversification but also an "increase of interest in theory and methodology".

On the other hand, the expansion of the field, resulting from the growth of organizational psychology, led other writers of that period to characterize organizational theory and research as lacking coherence and integration because of the different disciplinary perspectives and levels of analysis involved. Roberts, Hulin, & Rousseau (1978), for example, identify four social science paradigms: industrial-organizational psychology, human factors (or ergonomics), social psychology, and sociology, which underpin research and theory in this area, but which are rarely made explicit by researchers and practitioners, although it is these paradigms that determine the nature of theory, the variables and levels of analysis deemed to be important and the measures used. As a result, each paradigm leads to a focus on some units of analysis without reference to others, "individuals in industrial-organisational psychology, tasks in human factors studies, individuals in groups in social psychology, and groups and organisations in sociology" (Roberts et al., 1978, p.26). In their view, the effect of these disciplinary or subdisciplinary "filters" has been to prevent any effective aggregation of concepts and findings across the field as a whole because there is no integrating framework which effectively bridges the gaps between them. The separate strands can be seen clearly in the following outline of developments in W&O psychology in this phase of its history, but these show too that, in terms of practice and application, social values were as large, if not greater, determinants of the direction taken than research-based theory.

In the realm of personnel selection, the cleavage between the statistical and the clinical approaches continued, but the former tended to gain ground, and was further consolidated by the development of new tests, validation studies, criterion research, and sophisticated psychometric models. Experimental simulations of the complex skills required by operators in the fields of aviation, vehicle and marine transport, and space exploration formed part of a battery of selection procedures in some instances, as well as being used as training aids (Cassie, Fokkema, & Parry, 1964; Institute of Measurement and Control, 1977). And the clinical approach to selection appeared in a new garb in the "assessment centres" favoured increasingly as a means of selecting mangers and of identifying their long-term potential. Associated particularly with managerial appraisal in large companies in the USA, and pioneered by the American Telegraph and Telephone Company in 1956, an "assessment centre" refers to the use of multiple assessment techniques, at least one of which simulates important aspects of real job situations, by which an individual or group of individuals is assessed by a group of judges. Whereas America dominated research in this domain in the 1950s, from the 1960s onwards European psychologists began to make an increasing contribution, showing the value of this approach as a diagnostic instrument for career planning and management development, rather than advocating its use mainly as a selection device as in the USA (Seegers, 1989).

A move towards more humanistic forms of work organization and concomitant advocacy of the principles of self-determination as a means of regulating workplace behaviour were leading factors in many of the attempts to introduce planned organizational change in the 1960s. "T-groups" and sensitivity training sought to bring about changes in organizations by changing individuals who, through exploring the interpersonal processes occurring in an unstructured group setting, were enabled to develop more open and trusting behaviours. By the end of that decade, however, it was realized that these approaches had more effect on people's personal development than on daily organizational life and more task-related intervention techniques came to be used under the general rubric of *organization development* (OD). This term covers a broad range of change strategies designed to enhance both people and

organizations in the way they operate. As different practitioners have their own preferred orientations, OD in practice takes many forms, and is an area in which theory and ideology are perhaps more closely intertwined than elsewhere in W&O psychology. It is also a sphere in which practitioners may be well qualified in psychology or have had little formal training in the subject. A favoured method in OD programmes is "action research", whereby the research worker is also a consultant, taking a professional role in relation to the client system, rather than operating solely as a detached observer. Used originally in the Lewinian sense in the Anglo-American world, it was extended later by members of the Tavistock Institute to denote researcher and the various parties in the client-system agreeing jointly on the nature of the problem, the type of solution sought, and the methods used, together with the active involvement of the researcher in any implementation of the findings. On the Continent, Marxian thinking led to the development of a characteristic style of action research (*Handlungsforschung*) in some quarters.

The impetus to humanize and improve the *quality of working life*, which was instrumental in organizational change programmes centred on interpersonal and group relations processes, also led to a concentration on new approaches to job design in this period. As with OD, the various "paradigms of practice" (Van Strien, 1978) which were developed in this context were guided by a mixture of theory and ideology. Some of the theoretical components were derived from Herzberg's "motivator-hygiene" theory, which was influenced by Maslow's theory of motivation, and related experiments in the US with job enlargement and job enrichment. Other parts were taken from the socio-technical systems theory developed by Trist and others of the British Tavistock group, which advocated that, instead of dividing jobs into fragmented tasks, wherever possible autonomous work groups should be given responsibility for different 'whole tasks'. In addition, a psychological brand of *alienation theory* could also be discerned in the theoretical background of some job design activities. Common to all of these experiments was a change of orientation from one designed to control the behaviour of people at work to one that sought primarily to involve them in their jobs. Along with offering workers greater autonomy and more opportunity to develop their capabilities, re-structuring the workplace sought to stimulate democracy on the shop-floor.

At the same time, *industrial democracy* (ID) became a topic in its own right for some W&O psychologists, particularly those in Scandinavian countries where labour legislation gave workers and their unions a substantial role in organiza-tional decision making. Psychologists acted as consultants to Workers' Councils to assist them to exert their newly acquired legal rights. The form of codetermination and co-ownership then in operation in Yugoslavia provided another example, and there was a great interest in the position of workers in cooperatives. Here again, the underlying philosophy of the ID movement was a mixture of psychological theories of motiva-tion and political ideology.

Work psychologists in most Eastern European countries, in the wake of stalinist strictures on personnel selection, were concerned mainly with ergonomics, or engineering psychology as it is known in the USA (Leonova, 1994). In advanced countries across the globe, as in the war years, when the design of detection systems and other equipment stimulated developments in cognitive psychology, the demands of new and complex man–machine systems in this period drew upon and promoted new cognitive theories of percep-tion, memory, and control. This cognitive ergo-nomics continued to be a typical field of interdisciplinary cooperation.

Taken as a whole, the period shows a number of contradictory tendencies. On the one hand W&O psychology became more recognized as a distinct branch of psychology. On the other hand its boundaries remained indeterminate and its separ-ate components were not linked by an integrating conceptual framework. In some respects, its scien-tific and professional underpinnings were consoli-dated, but in other ways it was "a house divided" by vehement ideological debates and contro-versies about the nature and purpose of science and its intended beneficaries. Many practitioners encountered a divide between research endeav-ours and the practical problems with which they

were faced, so that only some of the developing theories became embodied in a viable *paradigm of practice*. In general, the emphasis was more on change than on explanation. Organizational characteristics became the focus of attention rather than individual responses, but the problem of how to relate these two levels of analysis conceptually or empirically was hardly tackled.

LATER DEVELOPMENTS

As in the past, the stage on which the present W&O psychologists are performing has as its back-cloth major political upheavals and changing configurations in the power structures within and between nations, Among those of recent note are the end of the Cold War, involving the collapse of the former soviet Union, the re-unification of Germany, turbulence and war in the Middle East and the Balkans, with concomitant economic and social consequences. There has been a world-wide economic recession, uneven in its impact and timing in different countries, but now also affect-ing Japan, once taken as the model of a highly successful modern economy. In the wake of this recession, according to the Organization for Econ-omic Cooperation and Development (OECD, 1994), unemployment is now widespread among the world's advanced industrial nations. In the second half of the 1990s there are signs that the international economic situation is recovering, but the attendant growth is mainly a jobless growth. How to create jobs to deal with this problem is an unresolved issue for national governments and international organizations alike. It underlies debates on political and economic affairs at all levels. In Europe, proposals to extend the EC and to move towards closer integration of the member States are other factors shaping the context in which W&O psychologists practise their pro-fession. How they have been, and are being, affected by the changing circumstances outlined above is the subject of this section.

New challenges and opportunities

Traditionally, the domain of W&O psychologists has been that of employment—advising people of their suitability for different kinds of work, selecting and training employees, analysing the nature of jobs and assisting in their design, including the social organization of work, motivating employees, and so on. With the increasing rates of change associated with technological innovation, they have been involved with programmes concerned with helping people to accept and to manage change in work organizations and to acquire new skills, but, until recently, unemployment and its effects were, almost by definition, outside the province of psychologists dealing with *work*. Now a growing number of them are engaged in unemployment-related activities, such as counselling individuals who have lost their jobs and helping them to decide whether to retrain or restructure their lives; with research into the personal and social consequences of unemployment; and with programmes to equip young people who have been unable to find employment to enter the job market. Others have focused on the differential employment opportunities available to different sectors of the population, particularly minority groups, and examined their implications for social policy.

In the realm of industry and commerce, the trends of the last decades of a shrinking manufacturing base and an expanding service sector have continued, with an increased emphasis on technological innovation to achieve economic survival and growth. As yet, these new technologies result in a reduction in the number of jobs available rather than an increase in them so that, while they may make an enterprise more effective and competitive, the people they displace represent an increased financial burden on the state. The emphasis in all spheres of employment is on achieving more with the same or fewer resources, frequently leading to organizational restructuring, closures, and mergers. As a result, there have been extended opportunities for practitioners specializing in "organizational change" consultancy, which includes, but is not restricted to, W&O psychologists.

Demands for the education and development of managers and administrators, on the one hand, and of information technology specialists, on the other, have accompanied these developments. Psychologists contribute to both these spheres, but in neither have they a monopoly of their subject, which may be taught in a multidisciplinary context by other social and behavioural scientists. Likewise, the tendency for a splitting to occur between theory and practice, referred to earlier, appears to continue unabated, with perhaps rather more interest in the money-earning potential of applied psychology on the part of academic institutions than formerly as they are encouraged to generate income to augment the limited financial provision from central funds.

Responses to these challenges

As indicated, clearly identifiable responses by work psychologists to the economic problems of recent years can be seen in their increased involvement with the individual and social consequences of unemployment, previously the concern primarily of social psychologists (Jahoda, 1982), and with the design of more flexible working time arrangements (Thierry & Meijman, 1994). At the interface with clinical psychology, some are engaged in stress counselling of those whose job demands and pressures threaten their health and well-being. Increasingly, attention is being paid to the nature and sources of stress in different occupations with regard both to the design of jobs and the selection of personnel for them (Amick & Ostberg, 1987). How to cope with the strain engendered by absence of work for many people and, conversely, with that experienced in their jobs by many others, exemplify the type of problems for which psychological help is currently being sought at the level of the individual.

Within organizations, whether manufacturing or providers of services, pressures to maintain or improve their position in rapidly changing and increasingly global markets have led to demands for adaptable staff and flexible organization structures and processes. In response, a lot of development work is taking place in organizations to which W&O psychologists are contributing, alongside other specialists. Depending on the needs of the situation, transient or permanent project teams may be involved, or a mixture of both, in determining how to achieve a better match between the human operator and the machine and between the people, technology, and organizational style, structures, and processes.

A notable feature of recent years has been the growth of networks and collaborative ventures by European work psychologists. 1976 saw the publication in the American journal *Personnel Psychology* of a review of industrial psychology in Europe, prompted by a request from its former editor, the late Rains Wallace, and prepared by a group of seven psychologists from different European countries. This was followed by a book (de Wolff et al., 1981) from the same group, with some additional contributions. In 1981 also, some 35 professors of W&O psychology from 15 different countries founded ENOP (European Network of Organizational and Work Psychologists), subsequently enlarged in its membership and representation, to explore together academic and professional issues in a European context. Two years later, the first North-Western European Conference on the Psychology of Work and Organization was held at Nijmegen, attended by over 200 psychologists, and followed by a second at Aachen in 1985. As the national psychological associations participating in these conferences extended beyond the original grouping of the Netherlands, the UK, West Germany, and Belgium, a European Association of Work and Organizational Psychology came into being which has now held international gatherings in 1987, 1989, 1991, 1993, 1995, and 1997 at Antwerp, Cambridge, Rouen, Alicante, Giör (Hungary), and Verona respectively. Other examples of the institutionalization of European exchanges and collaboration are the European Federation of Professional Psychological Associations (EFPPA) and the first European Congress of Psychology, held in Amsterdam in 1989, in which W&O psychologists, together with colleagues from other branches of the discipline, have taken an active part (Drenth, Sergeant, & Takens, 1990). This initiative was followed up by further biannual meetings in Budapest, Tampere, Athens, and Dublin. In addition, there has been a steady growth in staff and student exchanges and in collaborative research projects between countries, facilitated by the Erasmus programme and other funding schemes of the European Community. Some cross-national research studies have been on a very large scale, e.g. that on The Meaning of Working by the MOW International Research Team (1987) entailing eight national samples and ten target occupational groups. A new journal, published in association with the IAAP (International Association of Applied Psychology), appeared in 1991 entitled *The European Journal of Work and Organizational Psychology*. Another effect of the increasing international collaboration is the publication of international handbooks on W&O psychology such as the Handbook of Dunnette & Hough (1990–94) and the present handbook.

Paradigms of practice

As noted earlier, practice in W&O psychology is influenced to a large extent by values and only in part does it derive from research-based theory. Furthermore, there is often a separation between those engaged in academic research, who can remain detached from the problems of implementation, and practitioners concerned with strategies of intervention, for whom the question is what will work in the situation they face, but not the question of why it works.

This gap between research and organizational practices is, as Robertson (1989) notes, greater in some areas of W&O psychology than in others, and personnel selection is one in which it is relatively small. Citing the mathematical/statistical work on meta-analysis and validity generalization which suggests that many selection methods are more valid than previously thought, and that the validity of a method is not limited to one job or one situation, he argues that while neither has been accepted unreservedly by the scientific community, their impact on selection theory and research has been profound. It remains to be seen what effect it will have on practice.

In attempting to introduce organizational change, the focus of attention has moved over the years from organizational structure and processes to "organizational culture", seen by some as a form of human relations management in new guise (Hollway, 1991). Popularized, but not well defined conceptually, the term implies the embodiment of the belief systems and espoused values of top management in direct and symbolic ways, such as managerial style, language, rituals, and myths, which encourage identification with the organization and commitment to its goals on the part of employees. The claim is that change can be induced by shaping values and promoting a shared set of beliefs throughout an organization that will produce a consensus in line with changing organizational objectives.

Some perceive the thrust of psychological interventions, as distinct from those by more sociologically oriented practitioners, as aimed at the individual, often combined with an ideology of self-determination and self-regulation. From this perspective, stress too may be approached in terms of giving individuals techniques to control or avoid the experience of stress, rather than focusing on the structural factors that give rise to it. There has been a revival of interest in attribution theory (Furnham, Sadka, & Brewin, 1992, Jaspars, Hewstone, & Fincham, 1983), both in terms of people's judgements of others' perceptions and intentions and of self-attributions relating to success and failure, stress and anxiety, and the like.

Increasingly, however, W&O psychologists are dealing with problems of a complex order which have to be dealt with in a multidisciplinary context. This applies particularly in the design of technical systems and in equipment design, where the importance of moving from a machine-centred approach to a user-oriented approach is recognized, but knowledge of how to achieve it is still rudimentary. Designers and project managers are used to working to specifications related only to technological performance, with ergonomists and psychologists looking at the human and organizational implications of a piece of equipment or a working system only when its basic parameters have been set.

It is difficult to discern any unifying theory underlying W&O psychology at present. In academic psychological circles, one sees a tendency in some quarters to treat work psychology as applied experimental psychology and organizational psychology as applied social psychology, but there is also an applied behavioural science literature with a more eclectic emphasis favoured by those who teach in management and business schools. Among social science theorists, various radical critiques of the development and nature of work psychology have been advanced in recent years (Hollway, 1991, Rose, 1985; Thompson & McHugh, 1990). Currently, these are more widely known among sociologists than psychologists, but are not without influence on a minority of the latter. Of an entirely different order is the tide of consultancy and management publications, addressed to practitioners, advocating with missionary zeal a particular technique or approach to organizational problems as a universal panacea until that technique becomes, in turn, displaced by a new solution. Some well-known theories and concepts, such as Maslow's hierarchy of human needs and Herzberg's two-factor theory of the motivation to work, have been popularized in this way and incorporated in management thinking and discussion. The concept of corporate culture as presented by Peters and Waterman (1982) in *In Search of Excellence* is a more recent example.

These contrasting perspectives illustrate the long-standing dilemma inherent in W&O psychology as a practice profession, i.e. for whom and on whose behalf are the members employed. Some, with strong political views, have confined themselves to analytical critique and avoided active engagement with organizations; others have no problem with aligning themselves with a particular side; and yet others seek to put a ring around their activities as in devising tests without concerning themselves as to how they are to be used. Although professional cultures differ in and between countries, one of the functions of the cross-national exchanges and meetings referred to earlier is to reinforce the values of groups and subgroups within the profession as a whole.

THE DYNAMICS OF HISTORY

It is always tempting to judge the past in the light of the present norms (*presentism*), a tendency from which W&O psychologists are not immune. This results in the over-evaluation and approbation of past developments that anticipate current approaches, and a dismissive attitude towards theories and methods no longer in fashion. By describing developments as responses to challenges that vary from period to period, and recognizing the need of psychologists of any generation to make their work acceptable to their contemporaries, we have tried to make the reader aware of the (relative) sense of features of W&O psychology in the past which are hard to understand today. Thus, a society in which philosophical or political preconceptions dominated looked for a psychology in tune with these perspectives. Likewise, in a period in which in personnel selection assessment of the whole person was sought, rather than specific attributes, the use of projection tests, and even graphology, appears to be less aberrant then it seems from our present norms. Although psychologists who did not follow the mainstream of their time and anticipated later developments, belonging to an era of different challenges, may be "advanced" in our eyes, it is important to remember that our present views, in their turn, will be criticized by later generations. Not only the views of our predecessors but also our own are historically relative, in the sense of related to (= bound up with) problems which, in a changing society, are continuously changing. Many of the truths of today are the errors of tomorrow. Hence, acquiring a sense of historical relativity both brings us closer to the past and distances us from the present.

Does this relativity then enable us to speak of progress in our discipline over a period of time? Yes, insofar as some answers to presenting problems can be seen as more adequate to the problems at issue than others current at the time. No, insofar as we can only speak of progress when there is consensus on the criteria by which it is to be measured. Our judgements as scientists and practitioners are influenced by prevailing societal norms and values which, in retrospect, will be seen to be historically relative. But historical reflection can also help to guide present action if we focus on the *supra-personal dynamics* of the history of our subject. By looking at the structural factors which lead to the development of science it is possible, by a process analogous to the interpretation by a psychoanalyst of a patient's past, to learn lessons from history by acquiring a better insight into factors shaping the directions taken in theory and practice. Space does not permit of a detailed exposition of this process here, but the elements of it are encompassed in a model developed for this purpose by the second author in previous historical investigations (Van Strien, 1991, 1993), which is outlined below.

Scientists and their public: A multirelational model of the dynamics of history

In the preceding account of the emergence of W&O psychology, we have indicated the influence of new problems on the way the subject developed. In the phase in which the profession still had to establish itself, it was practical questions, relating to the deployment of human resources, that challenged the pioneers of the field first to use the methods and instruments developed in the psychological laboratory for the measurement of aptitudes, and subsequently to develop *tests* as the preferred tool of the new profession. There is a stream within the historiography of science, so-called *externalism*, that tends to ascribe new developments in general to external, socio-economic factors. It cannot be denied that much of the dynamics of the history of W&O psychology has been sparked by these kinds of external challenges and opportunities. This was particularly the case during the two world wars, and the social and economic changes that occurred in their aftermath. But in the course of history there have been also influences from within psychology as an academic discipline. The methodological reorientation in European psychology in the 1960s is an example of such an influence from the side of academic psychology. Another example is the present striving for theoretical integration.

Thus, the birth of a new science or profession and its subsequent development may be seen as a response to the challenge of new problems arising partly within the existing scientific culture and partly in the wider society. A new approach to these problems (e.g. testing for aptitude) is successful insofar as it is perceived by the "owners of the problem" as providing more satisfactory answers than those based on common sense or on the approach of already established sciences. These "problem owners" from whom questions arise and to whom the answers have to prove satisfactory form the "public" or "audience" of the new science. This public usually comprises a number of groups. In a practice-directed field such as W&O psychology, the predominant group consists of (potential) clients for the services of the profession, including governmental and other bodies which fund or sponsor research. Alongside this is the scientific and professional community of the scientist's own discipline, in this instance the psychological "establishment", and members of related disciplines (e.g. sociologists). Other interested parties in society at large (e.g. educated laymen and opinion leaders such as journalists and politicians) form another group. These various "publics" serve both as references for testing conceptual ideas and paradigms of practice and as a critical audience that has to be convinced of the soundness of the answers produced to the original problems if these are to become accepted and legitimized.

In its pioneer phase a new science or field of practice seldom has the command of its own, adequate tools for tackling the problems it sets itself to solve. Initially, the required methods and theoretical notions are borrowed from another, more advanced "exemplary" science or profession. In the "psychotechnical" phase this was natural science and technics. Work was conceived in a machine-like fashion, and the tests used in personnel selection were conceived as a kind of measuring rods. In the subsequent "holistic" psychology it was the organic life-sciences and, as far as psychodiagnostic practice is concerned, psychiatric diagnostics, that set the tune. Testing was remodelled from an interpretative perspective, and organizations were conceived as organic wholes. In more recent years it was the *information-processing* approach of modern cognitive science from which psychologists drew their inspiration.

The *paradigms of practice* that were developed on this basis were not just applications of existing theory, but originated in most cases, after some trial and error, from practical problem-solving situations, where they acquired the character of successful problem-solving repertoires (for example the human relations paradigm and the socio-technical paradigm). There are many instances in the history of psychology in which scientific theorizing (e.g. about intelligence) followed, rather than preceded, practical problem solving (Schönpflug, 1992; Snijders, 1969). Therefore, instead of speaking of applied psychology (the "top-down" view) it is more appropriate to speak of an *interaction between theory and practice*, which leaves room for "bottom-up" theory development. In addition to theoretical notions, "ideological" notions and images of man also play a role in paradigms of practice, for example the *economic man* of scientific management, *social man* of human relations thinking, and *man as a computer* in the information-processing approach.

Once established, the institutional arrangements, such as university laboratories, research institutes, journals, professional service organizations, which promote and develop the discipline depend for their continuation on the conviction of the relevant "publics" that the scientific problem solving entailed is successful and worthwhile. To this end, the "rhetoric" of science plays its part in convincing the public of the value of its contribution; that is, it is a two-way exchange in which psychologists, by popularizing their insights, to a certain extent create the demand for their services themselves. In the course of our century there has been a *psychologization* in the way people conceive their problems. It has induced the public no longer to rely on its own common-sense remedies, but rather to think of its difficulties as psychological problems, asking for expert advice and treatment. On the other hand, psychologists had to attune their approaches to the views that prevailed in the society of which they were a part (Dehue, 1991, 1995). In the context of this interplay, new developments or reorientations occurred as the result of changes in the "relational field" of scientists and professionals (Van Strien, 1991, 1993).

At any one time, this interplay between theory and practice and between science and society results in a set of problems and topics agreed to be the domain and method of working of an applied discipline. As Cherns (1982, p.25) observed, "the set changes over time less because the topics are exhausted and the problems solved, than because they are differently perceived" or, in our terminology, because changing images of man and changing values in society cause previously successful paradigms of practice to lose their vigour, and prompt the development of a new paradigm that accords better with these changing values. Seen in this way, the resultant "paradigm switch" in orientation and methods of working, of which we have cited examples from W&O psychology in earlier sections of this chapter (such as the replacement of scientific management by the human relations appproach, and the changing approaches to personnel selection), are not historical accidents but the outcome of the interplay of forces in the dynamic model just described.

The widening field: Some inherent dilemmas and conflicts

In its early days, W&O psychology was concerned with the application of the newly emergent discipline of psychology to the domain of work. As with the parent discipline, the unit of analysis was the individual, who was seen as the "object" of scientific enquiry by the psychologist, in a relationship derived from, and more akin to, that between experimenter and laboratory animal than between fellow human beings. Whether working in an academic setting or on behalf of an industrial organization, the psychologists concerned were dealing with relatively specific problems and occupying clearly defined roles as "scientists". Implicit in the latter were assumptions of impartiality, "objectivity", and detachment of the investigator as inherent properties of the scientific method.

In the intervening years, all this has changed. Not only has the field of W&O psychology diversified and extended, especially with the inclusion of organizations within its area of study, but the climate of opinion regarding science and professional practice has altered radically. Heisenberg's (1958) postulation of the "uncertainty principle" in physics, to the effect that scientific research involves an interaction between the scientist and the object of investigation, and that it is the nature of this interaction that determines what the scientist observes, heralded a longstanding debate about whether or not science is value free. In psychology, this led to a revival of interest in subjectivity and experiential approaches and, in some quarters, to a turning away from traditional scientific and positivistic methods of enquiry. Alongside the growth of social values that emphasize personal freedom and self-determination, the role of the psychologist as expert has been queried and rejected as untenable by those who believe in the value of joint exploration and accountability as, for example, in action research.

As we indicated earlier, it is the activities of practitioners that have received the most scrutiny and censure by advocates of a humanistic stance. Though their subject includes studies of the effects of payment systems on the attitudes and behaviour of workers, W&O psychologists have tended not to look at the way their own sources of income and allegiances influence their activities, except in the most general terms. It is accepted that consultants have to persuade would-be clients that it is worth their while to employ them and that, in consequence, they may be tempted to become primarily marketeers, selling social science "packages" as solutions to clients' problems without subjecting these to diagnosis and detailed investigation, a situation from which professional codes of practice seek to protect clients. But even the most scrupulous professionals are often caught in a dilemma in which they are pressed by clients to deal with problems outside their sphere of competence, or provide short-term, expedient answers for powerful interest groups, at variance with both their scientific training and their ethical principles.

The salaried academic, in theory, is untroubled by conflicts of this kind and free to respond to questions and problems posed by fellow scientists, as well as usually staying free from the pressure to generate answers within a given period of time. But, as academic institutions have become more dependent for their research activities on sponsored research, from private as well as public organizations, it is apparent that the scientists concerned are not immune from the charge that it is the interests of their sponsors rather than the advancement of the discipline that determines the nature of their endeavour. "Ear-marked" funds by government agencies for particular projects have been known to invoke competitive tendering from those with no previous interest in the topic and, while any commissioned project usually entails negotiation between sponsors and researchers, in their eagerness to obtain the contract the latter may be unwilling to consider the political and ethical dimensions involved. For example, policy makers may commission research in order to delay making a decision they wish to avoid, but by initiating the project they raise expectations that the issues in question will be taken seriously.

It is customary for research to be a delegated activity, using assistants paid for out of grants or contracts, on the obtaining of which the researcher's academic reputation, the continued employment of the research assistants and, perhaps, ultimately the survival of the research institution may depend. As a result, heads of departments and research directors may feel they must engage in political activity in the form of cultivating sponsors and grant-awarding bodies. This is perhaps a less blatant "selling operation" than occurs in consultancy, but the underlying questions of social responsibility and accountability are of the same order. In both situations, psychologists are expected to serve the needs and conform with the values of different groups (or "publics" in the terminology of the model described earlier), which may be incompatible at best and, at worst, irreconcilable.

Since the 1970s there has been much discussion of issues of this kind, linked with debate about the extent to which the scientific study of human behaviour, particularly in the realm of organizations, inevitably serves the interests of the most powerful members because psychologists employed in and by organizations have to engage with the prevailing system if they are to operate at all. How far they accommodate to its norms and values or are able to shape the situation to accord with their own will vary with each individual and each engagement. Whatever guidance they may receive from their fellow professionals, which, according to Mirvis & Seashore (1982), is usually far from adequate, ultimately it rests with the individual psychologist to define his or her standards of professional conduct.

Even so, this may be difficult to achieve in a field in which psychologists can find that their efforts, say, to improve the quality of working life are misconstrued by the potential beneficiaries as forms of manipulation and control. Programmes of joint consultation and the humanization of work may, as Van Strien (1978) suggests, in reality serve as a barrier against any fundamental redistribution of power in the organization, although the psychologists concerned do not perceive this. In his view, the appropriate stance for psychologists

in these circumstances is to make clear to the workers that the aim of the programme is to make better use of the organization's human resources and let them decide whether or not to enter the game (assuming they are free to do so).

Where do we go from here?

We have argued that history does not repeat itself, but that an appreciation of the history of work and organizational psychology encourages a more reflective stance on present developments and the factors to be considered by W&O psychologists if they wish to survive as a successful profession. Of prime importance here is sensitivity to new challenges and opportunities in our environment, particularly the changing nature of work and employment.

From the early days of industrial psychology onwards, it has been assumed that "earning a living" in the so-called "developed" societies of the world entailed employment on a full-time basis in enterprises outside the home. Also, that people would follow a given occupation throughout their working lives. Hence, the main thrust of psychologists' activities in this sphere has always been to achieve the best fit between the needs of employers, in terms of their personnel requirements, and the needs and aspirations of those seeking employment. Over the years, social, technological, economic, and political changes have led to marked changes in the content and patterns of work, for example the increased participation of women in the labour force and the demands for equal opportunities, the development of information technology and its applications such as "tele-working" and computer conferencing, the decline of manufacturing and the growth of service industries, direct and indirect intervention by government agencies designed to control working practices such as health and safety regulations. Where these changes have been incremental, W&O psychologists have been able to accommodate their professional activities to new circumstances and have not perceived them as a threat to their area of practice, largely due to the many subspecialisms in the field. For example, those who are concerned with the selection and assessment of managers do not, as a rule, operate in the area of organizational design, and those who focus on ergonomics rarely, if ever, deal with the problems of racial discrimination in employment.

The question now is whether this "accommodation by fragmentation" will be sufficient for professional survival in the future, not least because of the increasing complexity of, and interactions between, the different parts of the domain. This is most evident in relation to systems of advanced technology, where technology is not only an independent variable, affecting the skills, tasks, roles, careers, group functioning, departmental and management structure on the organisation in which it is introduced, but is also a dependent variable, shaped by the knowledge, skills, values, roles, relationships, career paths, etc. in the organizations where it is designed. Pressure is increasing for an integrated approach to technology, organization, and human factors in the creation of effective operational structures, but this requires a holistic perception of people doing work and the willingness and ability of psychologists to collaborate with engineers and technologists from the initial design stage, for which no preparation is given to students in the academic training programmes of any of these disciplines. Among psychologists, the situation is compounded by the split between those who see themselves as predominantly scientists and those who perceive themselves mostly as practitioners, the former concentrating on research in the academic mode and the latter on problem solving on behalf of clients. It is a divide of long standing, on which Dunnette (1990) reflects in the opening chapter of the second edition of his *Handbook of Industrial and Organisational Psychology*, noting that in the first edition in 1976 he was optimistic that a fusion between science and practice was emerging, but that schisms have continued because of institutional factors that serve to perpetuate the division. Chief among these, in his opinion, are "reward systems in both academic and nonacademic settings that emphasise short-run accomplishments as contrasted with more thoughtful, larger, and more thorough enhancements to the overall knowledge base of the field" (pp.2–16). The academic is under pressure to "publish or perish" and the practitioner to promote activities or techniques as panaceas for all kinds of organizational problems. To counter such ten-

dencies, it will be necessary to redefine the criteria of occupational success for W&O psychologists, giving more credit for joint and collaborative work with others and judging research in organizational settings in terms of its applicability and implementation.

With regard to employment opportunities, it can no longer be assumed that people will aspire to, or achieve an opening that provides, a job or career "for life". Partly as a result of economic recession, partly through technological developments that make some skills and occupations obsolete, and partly because of a tendency by some large companies to move jobs to developing countries where labour is cheap and plentiful, job security is an increasingly scarce phenomenon in advanced industrial societies. There are increasingly large numbers of school leavers, with few or no qualifications, who are unable to get a job at all, and older employees at all levels who are made redundant, offered early retirement and/or in various ways encouraged or compelled to change their occupation or opt out of the labour market in the course of their working lives. Furthermore, an increasing amount of work is now subcontracted by large organizations in order to reduce central staff costs and overheads, creating both a cadre of self-employed professional workers, who sell their services on a consultancy basis, and a pool of unskilled, peripheral workers with little bargaining power, engaged on a casual basis. In these circumstances, W&O psychologists have the chance to extend their range to the selection of unskilled, casual, and seasonal workers about which, as Cook (1989) pointed out, we know next to nothing; likewise, to considering how the contracting organization can or should assess the suitability of self-employed professionals (Hollway, 1991). Both these issues challenge the conventional thinking in W&O psychology on organizational attachment and the desirability of developing people's subjective ties to a work organization, and relate more to an individualistic than to a collectivist perspective.

There is a latent conflict of values to be noted here, to which the chapter on Personnel Selection in the 1992 Annual Review of Psychology draws attention. Speaking of the United States, it observes that research has not, and cannot, "resolve the conflict between competing American values of individual merit, economic efficiency and international competitiveness on the one hand, and economic equality and opportunities for minorities, on the other" (Schmidt, Ones, & Hunter, 1992, p.662) and poses the question as to whether it will remain possible, politically and legally, to use valid selection procedures "in our litigious and multi-cultural society" (Schmidt, Ones, & Hunter, 1992, p.662). Even if such fears prove to be ill-founded, there is no doubt that the contexts in which psychological methods of personnel selection are used are now politically more sensitive than they were formerly. Addressing the same question from a European perspective, Drenth (1989) proposes some strategies for the maximization of equal opportunities in selection. It is clear that in this precarious situation psychologists, like other professionals such as medical practitioners, must be prepared to be publically accountable for their actions.

REFERENCES

Allport, G.W., & Vernon, P.E. (1931). *A test for personal values*. Boston: Houghton Mifflin.

Amick, B.C., & Östberg, O. (1987). Office automation, occupational stress and health. *Office: Technology and People*, *3*, 191–209.

Baritz, L. (1960). *The servants of power: A history of the uses of the social sciences in American industry*. Middletown, CN: Wesleyan University Press.

Baumgarten, F. (1928). *Die Berufseignungsprüfungen; Theorie und Praxis*. München: Oldenbourg.

Baumgarten, F. (Ed.) (1949). *Progrès de la Psycho-techique*. Bern: Francke.

Bennis, W., Benne, K.D., & Chin, W. (Eds) (1969). *The planning of change*. New York: Holt, Rinehart & Winston.

Biegel, R.A. (1938). *Rapport betreffende een onderzoek over kleurcombinaties en indeling van nummerbor-den*. Tijdschrift Wegen.

Binet, A., & Simon, T. (1905). Methodes nouvelles pour le diagnostic du niveau intellectuel des abnormeaux. *L'Annee Psychologique*, *14*, 141–244.

Block, N.J., & Dworkin, G. (Eds) (1976). *The I.Q. controversy*. New York: Random House.

Blum, M.L., & Naylor, J.C. (1968). *Industrial psychology*. New York: Harper & Row.

Broadbent, D.E. (1958). *Perception and Communication*. Oxford, UK: Pergamon.

Broadbent, D.E. (1961). *Behaviour*. London: Eyre & Spottiswoode.

Bures, Z. (1991). Psychology of work in Czechoslovakia. *The Occupational Psychologist*, *15*, 3–14.

Carey, A. (1967). The Hawthorne studies: A radical criticism. *American Sociological Review*, *32*, 403–416.

Cassie, A., Fokkema, S.D., & Parry, J.B. (Eds) (1964). *Aviation psychology*. Den Haag: Mouton & Co.

Cattell, J.M. (1890). Mental tests and their measurement. *Mind*, *15*, 373–380.

Cherns, A.B. (1982). Culture and values: The reciprocal influence between applied social science and its cultural and historical context. In N. Nicholson & T.D. Wall (Eds.), *The theory and practice of organisational psychology* (pp.19–35). London: Academic Press.

Cook, M. (1989). Selection of operatives, manual, casual and seasonal workers. In P. Herriot (Ed.), *Assessment and selection in organisations* (pp.493–510). London: Wiley.

Craik, K.J.W. (1947). Theory of the human operator in control systems: Vol. 1. The operator as an engineering system. *British Journal of Psychology*, *38*, 56–61.

Craik, K.J.W. (1948). Theory of the human operator in control systems: Vol. 2. Man as an element in a control system. *British Journal of Psychology*, *38*, 142–148.

Darwin, C. (1859). *The origin of species*. London: John Murray.

Davis, L.E., & Cherns, A.B. (1975). *The quality of working life (Vol. 1)*. New York: Free Press.

de Wolff, C.J., & Shimmin, S. (1976). The psychology of work in Europe: A review of a profession. *Journal of Personnel Psychology*, *29*, 175–195.

de Wolff, C.J., Shimmin, S., & de Montmollin, M. (1981). *Conflicts and contradictions—work psychologists in Europe*. London: Academic Press.

Dehue, G.C.G. (1991). Transforming psychology in the Netherlands: Vol. I: Why methodology changes. *History of the human sciences*, *7*, 335–349.

Dehue, G.C.G. (1995). *The rules of the discipline: Dutch psychologists and their methodology 1900–1985*. New York: Cambridge University Press.

Dorsch, F. (1963). *Geschichte und Probleme der angewandten Psychologie*. Bern: Huber.

Drenth, P.J.D. (1987). Conclusions and further perspectives. In B.M. Bass & P.J.D. Drenth (Eds.), *Advances in organisational psychology* (pp.266–276). Beverly Hills, CA: Sage.

Drenth, P.J.D. (1989). Psychological testing and discrimination. In P. Herriot (Ed.), *Assessment and selection in organisations* (pp.71–80). London: Wiley.

Drenth, P.J.D., Sergeant, J.A., & Takens, R.J. (Eds) (1990). *European perspectives in psychology*. Chichester: Wiley.

DuBois, P.H. (1970). *A history of psychological testing.* Boston: Allyn & Bacon.

Dunnette, M.D. (1976). *Handbook of industrial and organisational psychology.* Chicago: Rand McNally.

Dunnette, M.D. (1990). Blending the science and practice of industrial and organizational psychology; where are we and where are we going. In M.D. Dunnette, & L.M. Hough (Eds), *Handbook of Industrial and Organizational Psychology*, (Vol. 1, pp.1–27). Palo Alto, CA: Consulting Psychologists Press.

Dunnette, M.D., Hough, L.M., & Triandis, H.C. (Eds) (1990–1994). Handbook of industrial and organisational psychology, (2nd ed; Vols 1–4). Palo Alto, CA: Consulting Psychologistis Press.

Edholm, O.G., & Murrell, H. (1974). *History of the ergonomics research society.* London: Taylor & Francis.

Emery, F.E., & Thorsrud, E. (1969). *Form and content in industrial democracy.* London: Tavistock Publications.

European Productivity Agency (1958). *Fitting the job to the worker: A survey of American and European research into working conditions in industry.* Project No. 335. Paris: OECD.

Frisby, C.B. (1970). The development of industrial psychology at the NIIP. *Occupational Psychology, 44,* 35–50.

Furnham, A., Sadka, V., & Brewin, C.R. (1992). The development of an Occupational Attributional Style Questionnaire. *Journal of Organisational Behaviour, 13,* 27–39.

Galton, F. (1883). *Inquiries into human faculties.* London: Macmillan.

Geuter, U. (1992). *The professionalisation of psychology in Nazi-Germany.* New York: Cambridge University Press. (Original work published in German 1984).

Gilbreth, F.B. (1911). *Motion study.* New York: Van Nostrand.

Gillespie, R. (1991). *Manufacturing knowledge: A history of the Hawthorne Experiment.* Cambridge, MA: Cambridge University Press.

Hearnshaw, L.S. (1964). *A short history of British psychology 1840–1940.* London: Methuen.

Heisenberg, W. (1958). *Physics and philosophy.* New York: Harper.

Hermann, T. (1966). Zur Geschichte der Berufseignungsdiagnostik (Sammelreferat) *Archiv für die gesamte Psychologie, 118,* 253–278.

Hinrichs, P. (1981). *Um die Seele des Arbeiters; Arbeitspsychologie, Industrie- und Betriebssoziologie in Deutschland.* Köln: Pahl-Rügenstein.

Hollway, W. (1991). *Work psychology and organisational behaviour—managing the individual at work.* London: Sage.

IDE-International Research Group (1981). *Industrial democracy in Europe.* Oxford, UK: Oxford University Press.

Institute of Measurement and Control (1977). *Human operators and simulation.* Collected papers from a symposium co-sponsored by the Ergonomics Society and the Institution of Electrical Engineers. London: Author.

Jaeger, S., & I. Staeuble (1981). Die Psychotechnik und ihre gesellschaftlichen Entwicklungsbedingungen. In *Die Psychologie des 20. Jahrhunderts. Band XIII* (pp.54–95). Zürich: Kindler.

Jahoda, M. (1982). *Employment and unemployment—a social-psychological analysis.* Cambridge, UK: Cambridge University Press.

Jaques, E. (1951). *The changing culture of a factory.* London: Tavistock Publications.

Jaspars, J., Hewstone, M., & Fincham, F.D. (1983). *Attribution theory and research: Conceptual, developmental, and social dimensions.* London: Academic Press.

Kelly, E.L., & Fiske, D.W. (1951). *The prediction of performance in clinical psychology.* Ann Arbor, MI: University of Michigan Press.

Kraepelin, E. (1896). Der psychologische Versuch in der Psychiatrie. *Psychologische Arbeiten, 1,* 1–91.

Kraepelin, E. (1902). Die Arbeitskurve. *Philosophische Studien, 19,* 459–507.

Lahy, J.M. (1927). *La sélection psychofysiologique des travailleurs, conducteurs de tramways et d'autobus.* Paris: Dunot.

Lasch, C. (1979). *The culture of narcissism.* New York: Norton.

Leonova, A.B. (1994). Industrial and organisational psychology in Russia. In C.L. Cooper & I.T. Robinson (Eds.), *International review of industrial and organisational psychology, Vol. 9* (pp.183–212). Chichester, UK: Wiley.

Lévy-Leboyer, C. (1988). Presidential address: 21st International Congress of Applied Psychology. *Applied Psychology, 37,* 95–96.

Lewin, K. (1947). Frontiers in group dynamics. *Human Relations, 1,* 5–41, 143–153.

Lewin, K. (1948). *Resolving social conflicts.* New York: Harper & Row.

Likert, R. (1961). *New patterns of management.* New York: McGraw-Hill.

Mackworth, N.H. (1956). Work design and training for future industrial skills. *Journal of the Institute of Production Engineering, 35,* 214–228.

Mayo, E. (1933). *The human Problems of an industrial civilisation.* New York: Viking.

Mirvis, P.H. & Seashore, S.E. (1982). Creating ethical relationships in organisational research. In J.E. Sieber (Ed.), *The ethics of social research* (pp.79–104). New York: Springer.

Mosso, A. (1904). *La Fatica* (Transl. M. & W.B. Drummond). London, UK: Swan Sonnenschein. (Original work published 1890).

MOW International Research Team (1987). *The meaning of working.* London: Academic Press.

Münsterberg, H. (1907). *On the witness stand.* New York: McClare.

Münsterberg, H. (1909). *Psychology and the teacher.* New York: Appleton & Co.

Münsterberg, H. (1912). *Psychologie und Wirtschaftsleben.* Leipzig: Barth.

Münsterberg, H. (1913). *Psychology and industrial efficiency.* Boston: Houghton Mifflin.

Münsterberg, H. (1914). *Grundzüge der Psychotechnik.* Leipzig: Barth

Murray, D.J. (1983). *A history of Western psychology.* Englewood Cliffs, NJ: Prentice-Hall.

Murrell, K.F.H. (1965). *Ergonomics: Man in his working environment.* London: Chapman & Hall.

Napoli, D.S. (1981). *Architects of adjustment: The history of the psychological profession in the United States.* Port Washington, WI: Kennikat Press.

OECD (1994). *The OECD jobs study: Facts, analysis, strategies.* Paris: Author.

OSS-Assessment Staff (1948). *Assessment of men.* New York: Rinehart.

Peiro, J.M. (1985). Some perspectives of work and organisational psychology in Spain. *B.P.S. Occupational Psychology Newsletter, 18,* 27–47.

Peiro, J.M., & Munduate, L. (1994). Work and organisational psychology in Spain. *Applied Psychology, 43,* 231–274.

Peters, T.J., & Waterman, R.H. (1982). *In search of excellence—lessons from America's best-run companies.* New York: Harper & Row.

Pugh, D.S., & Hickson, D.J. (1976). *Organisational structure in its context: The Aston programme.* Westmead: Saxon House.

Roberts, K.H., Hulin, C.L., & Rousseau, D.M. (1978). *Developing an interdisciplinary science of organizations* (pp.489–492). San Francisco: Jossey-Bass.

Robertson, I.T. (1989). Selection in specific occupational areas. In P. Herriot (Ed.), *Assessment and selection in organisations* (pp.439–492). Chichester, UK: Wiley.

Robertson, I.T., & Cooper, C.L. (1983). *Human behaviour on organisations.* Plymouth, UK: McDonald & Evans.

Rose, N. (1985). *The psychological complex; Psychology, politics and society in England 1869–1939.* London: Routledge.

Schmidt, F.L., Ones, D.S., & Hunter, J.E. (1992). Personnel Selection. In M.R. Rosenzweig & L.W. Porter (Eds.). *Annual Review of Psychology,* (pp.637–670). Palo Alto, CA: Annual Reviews Inc.

Schönpflug, W. (1992). Applied psychology: Newcomer with a long tradition. *Applied Psychology, 42,* 5–30.

Scott, W.D. (1903). *The theory of advertizing.* Boston: Small & Maynard.

Scott, W.D. (1908). *The psychology of advertizing.* Boston: Small & Maynard.

Scott, W.D. (1911). *Influencing men in business.* New York: Ronald Press

Seegers, J.J.J.L. (1989). Assessment centres for identifying long term potential and for self-development. In P. Herriot (Ed.), *Assessment and selection in organisations* (pp.745–771). Chichester, UK: John Wiley.

Shimmin, S. (1980). Industrial and organisational psychology in Britain, In X. Zamek-Gliszczynska (Ed.), *Work psychology in Europe* (pp.115–126). Warsaw: Polish Academy of Sciences.

Shimmin, S. (1986). History and natural history in occupational psychology. *Occupational Psychology Newsletter, 21,* 38–42.

Shimmin, S., & Wallis, D. (1994). *Fifty years of occupational psychology in Britain.* Leicester, UK: BPS Division and Section of Occupational Psychology.

Simoneit, M. (1943). *Grundriss der characterologischen Diagnostik.* Leipzig: Teubner.

Smith, M. (1945). *An introduction to industrial psychology.* London: Cassell.

Snijders, J.T. (1969). Interaction of theory and practice. *Nederlands Tijdschrift voor de Psychologie, 24,* 1–10.

Spaltro, E. (1980). Industrial and organisational psychology in Italy: The situation in 1978. In X. Zamek-Gliszezynska (Ed.), *Work psychology in Europe* (pp.143–158). Warsaw, Poland: Polish Academy of Sciences.

Spearman, C. (1904). General intelligence objectively measured and determined. *American Journal of Psychology, 15,* 201–293

Spearman, C. (1923). *The nature of intelligence and the principles of cognition.* London: Macmillan.

Stern, W. (1900). *Ueber Psychologie der individuellen Differenzen, Ideen zu einer differentiellen Psychologie.* Leipzig: Barth.

Stern, W. (1903). Angewandte Psychologie. *Beiträge zur Psychologie der Aussage, 1,* 4–45.

Stouffer, S.A. et al. (1949). *The American soldier* (Vols. 1 and 2). Princeton, NJ: Princeton University Press.

Strien, P.J. van (1976). Professional ethics and the quality of working life. In P. Warr (Ed.), *Personal goals and work design* (pp.127–139). London: Wiley.

Strien, P.J. van (1978). Paradigms in organisational research and practice. *Journal of Occupational Psychology, 56,* 291–300.

Strien, P.J. van (1991). Transforming psychology in the Netherlands: Vol. II. Audiences, alliances and the dynamics of change. *History of the Human Sciences, 4,* 351–369.

Strien, P.J. van (1993). The historical practice of theory construction. In H.V. Rappard, P.J. van Strien, L.P. Mos, & W.J. Baker (Eds), *Theory and history: Annals of theoretical psychology, Vol. VIII* (pp.149–228). New York: Plenum Press.

Strien, P.J. van (1994). *From the laboratory to the outside world: The theoretical assumptions of early psychotechnics.* Paper presented at the 13th Congress of the Cheiron European Society for the History of the Behavioural and Social Sciences, Paris, September.

Strien, P.J., van, de Wolff, C.J., & Takens, R.J. (1987). The Netherlands, In R. Gilgen & C. Gilgen (Eds), *International handbook of psychology* (pp.324–346). New York: Greenwood Press.

Strien, P.J. van (1997). Die psychotechnische Verwendung von Laboratoriumgeräten. In D. Albert & H. Gundlach (1997). *Apparative Psychologie; Geschichtliche Entwicklung und gegenwärtige Bedeutung.* Lengerich: Pabst Science Publishers.

Taylor, F.W. (1911). *The principles of scientific management.* New York: Harper.

Thierry, H., & Meijman, T.F. (1994). Time and behavior at work. In H.C. Triandis, M.D. Dunnette, & L.M. Hough (Eds), *Handbook of industrial and organisational psychology* (2nd ed., Vol. IV pp.341–413). Palo Alto, CA: Consulting Psychologists Press.

Thompson, P., & McHugh, D. (1990). *Work organisations; A critical introduction.* London: Macmillan.

Thorndike, E.L. (1927). *The measurement of intelligence.* New York: Teacher's College, Columbia University.

Thorndike, R.L. (1949). *Personnel selection.* New York: Wiley.

Thurstone, L.L. (1938). *Primary mental abilities.* Chicago: University of Chicago Press.

Trist, E.L., Higgin, G.W., Murray, H., & Pollock, A.B. (1963). *Organizational choice: Capabilities of groups or the cool face under changing technologies.* London: Tavistock Publications.

Veldkamp, T.A., & Drunen, P. van (1988). *Psychologie als professie*; *50 jaar Nederlands Instituut van Psychologen.* Assen: Van Gorcum.

Vernon, P.E., & Parry, J.B. (1949). *Personnel selection in the British Forces.* London: University of London Press.

Welch, H.J., & Myers, C.S. (1932). *Ten years of industrial psychology.* London: Pitman & Sons.

Wilpert, B. (1990). How European is work and organisational psychology? In P.J.D. Drenth, J.A. Sergeant, & R.J. Takens (Eds.), *European perspectives in psychology, Vol. III* (pp.3–20). Chichester, UK: Wiley.

Wyatt, F., & Teuber, H.L. (1944). German psychology and the Nazi-system 1933–1940. *Psychological Review, 51,* 229–247.

Yerkes, R.M. (1918). Psychology in relation to the war. *Psychological Review, 25,* 85–115.

Author Index

Subject Index